St. *Stephen's Green*

DOLMEN TEXTS 6

A Prospect of St Stephens Green

From Charles Brooking's map,
"A Prospect of the City of Dublin", *1728.*

St. Stephen's-Green

OR

The Generous Lovers

by

WILLIAM PHILIPS

Edited by

CHRISTOPHER MURRAY

UNIVERSITY COLLEGE DUBLIN

THE DOLMEN PRESS
North America: Humanities Press Inc.

*Set in Baskerville type
and printed and published in the Republic of Ireland
at the Dolmen Press
Mountrath, Portlaoise
in association with
Humanities Press Inc.
171 First Avenue, Atlantic Highlands,
New Jersey 07716, U.S.A.*

First published 1980

ISBN 0 85105 367 x The Dolmen Press

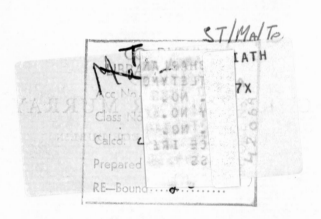

CONTENTS

ACKNOWLEDGMENTS

I wish to thank Mr Donal Looney of the National Library of Ireland for his help and consideration while I was at work on this edition; also Miss Dowd and Miss Egan of Dublin City Libraries, Pearse Street; Mr A. J. Flavell, Bodleian Library; Miss Mary Pollard, Trinity College Library, Dublin; and the staff of the library at University College, Dublin.

Many people were helpful in answering letters of enquiry, and I should especially like to thank D. Preston, librarian, Londonderry Divisional Headquarters; G. S. Slater, Public Record Office of Northern Ireland; L. M. Montgomery, librarian, Worcester College, Oxford; Mr Carey S. Bliss, curator, Huntington Library; Canon G. W. A. Knowles, Limavady; Professor T. W. Moody, Trinity College, Dublin; Professor J. C. Beckett, Queen's University, Belfast; Diana de Marly, Courtauld Institute; and Mr Roger Fiske, author of *English Theatre Music in the Eighteenth Century*.

In addition, I wish to thank Mr Alf MacLochlainn, Director, National Library of Ireland, for permission to reproduce the title page of *St Stephen's Green*.

Finally, my thanks to the general editor of *Irish Writings from the Age of Swift*, Dr Andrew Carpenter, whose encouragement and advice I deeply appreciate.

INTRODUCTION

I WILLIAM PHILIPS

FOR some time now the general view has persisted that Irish drama before the nineteenth century was scarcely worthy of attention. It has been said more than once that since drama was not an indigenous form the Irish people outside Dublin for the most part ignored it. The Irish literary artist seems to have found it more natural to express himself in poetry or in tale, rather than in the form of drama. Theatre, indeed, was a colonial manifestation, rooted in the towns founded by the invaders. As time went on, theatre occupied a significant place in the cultural life of the capital, the second city of the kingdom, where the Parliament sat and where the Lord Lieutenant presided over his little court. This was, of course, within the Pale, very far away from the problems of the peasantry.

The Pale, however, was hardly an iron curtain. Irish men passed in and out of Dublin, and some even stayed and wrote plays. To dismiss such plays as merely colonial is, it might be argued, to dispense with a part of that tangled web the Irish (or Anglo-Irish) literary tradition. It may well be that the picture we have of the Irish literary tradition, and in particular of the place of drama within that tradition, is too exclusive. Many years ago Dr Peter Kavanagh tried to broaden that picture in his survey of Irish-born playwrights, *The Irish Theatre* (1946), while more recently Professor David Krause has made room for Boucicault as forerunner of the Irish dramatic movement.[1] The time may be ripe now for a study of a single play from the beginnings of Ireland's dramatic history. *St Stephen's Green* is an example of a play written specifically for the Dublin stage, and it repays attention not only for historical

1. David Krause, "The Theatre of Dion Boucicault", *The Dolmen Boucicault* (Dublin : Dolmen Press, 1964), pp. 9–47.

reasons (as a specimen of late Restoration comedy, for example) but also as an introduction to the field of Irish theatre.

Surprisingly little is known about William Philips, the author of *St Stephen's Green*. He was a member of a prominent family, his great-grandfather, Sir Thomas Philips, having been a servitor under the crown during Hugh O'Neill's rebellion at the end of the sixteenth century.[2] He was rewarded with lands around Coleraine, and after the plantation of Ulster began he acquired the O'Cahan Castle at Limavady, together with three thousand acres. It was under his aegis that Newtown Limavady was built and was given a charter (in 1613) with the right of returning two members to the Irish Parliament. Sir Thomas's son Dudley (b. 1610) was the father of George Philips, the famous Governor of Derry who advised the Apprentice Boys to shut the gates against Lord Antrim's officers in 1688.[3] On 23 March 1689 Philips was sent to London with an address to King William and instructions to "Sollicit a speedy Supply" of ammunition and other necessaries.[4] While these supplies arrived in Derry on April 15, four days before the siege began, Philips himself stayed on in London where he published a pamphlet entitled *The Interest of England in the Preservation of Ireland*. In the course of his tocsin, Philips makes use of a

2. T. W. Moody, "Sir Thomas Phillips of Limavady, Servitor", *Irish Historical Studies*, I, No. 3 (March 1939), 251–72.
3. Richard Bagwell, *Ireland under the Stuarts and during the Interregnum*, vol. III *1660–1690* (London : Longmans, 1916), p. 190.
4. *The Siege of Londonderry, in 1689, as Set Forth in the Literary Remains of Colonel the Rev. George Walker, D.D.*, ed. Philip Dwyer (London and Dublin, 1893), p. 14; Rev. John Graham, *Derriana, Consisting of A History of the Siege of Londonderry* (Londonderry, 1823), p. 34. See also *DNB*, XV, 1060.

theatrical image, which possibly betrays an interest in the stage to be inherited by his son William : "I wish the good people of *England* may see in the Mirror of our Misfortunes, that Scheme of *Misery* and *Confusion* which was prepared for them, and which assuredly will be re-acted on their *Theatre*, if ever the *French* and *Irish* be permitted to *tread the Stage*." [5]

Strangely enough, Philips was ruined by the wars of 1689–90, in spite of being on the winning side, and he sold the manor at Limavady in 1691. Yet a letter dated 13 January 1691 indicates that he had returned to Derry and resumed some kind of official powers. The letter is to William King, the newly appointed Bishop of Derry, and it gives notice that Philips would appear in Derry on Thursday 21 January "to hear, & Examin the Matters Complained off by the Mayor of Londonderry to the Lds Justices." [6] Furthermore, a letter to Lord Capel dated 19 July 1694 indicates that Philips took part in the short-lived Irish Parliament of 1692.[7] Having been re-elected for the County of Londonderry on 8 August 1695 George Philips died, probably at the end of 1696, and on 17 April 1697 Captain William Philips was elected Burgess of Limavady in his place.[8] This is the first reference to the author of *St Stephen's Green* to be found.

5. *The Interest of England in the Preservation of Ireland. Humbly Presented to the Parliament of England. By G.P. Esq.* (London, 1689), p. 6.
6. MS. 201, Trinity College Library, Dublin. The letter is signed 'G Philips'. The catalogue states the recipient to be William King.
7. *Historical Manuscripts Commission. Report of the Manuscripts of the Duke of Buccleuch & Queensberry*, vol. II, Part I (London, 1903), pp. 104–5.
8. E. M. F. Boyle, *Records of the Town of Limavady. 1609 to 1808* (Londonderry, 1912), p. 40.

John Gilbert, presumably the 'J. T. G.' behind the *DNB* entry for William Philips, says that at an early age Philips "applied himself to writing for the stage." [9] It would be interesting to know the basis for this remark, since the date of Philips's birth is unknown. His first play, *The Revengeful Queen*, was staged at Drury Lane in June 1698.[10] In the Prologue to that play there is a suggestion that Philips had begun his career as a writer of songs:

> *He struggl'd long against his Muse's force,*
> *(Jades are more headstrong, than a Well-bred Horse)*
> *His* Phillis *first, by Songs, he try'd to move,*
> *Two curst Diseases, Poetry and Love!*
> *And having once giv'n loose to her dull Rage,*
> *She now has Impudence to mount the Stage.*[11]

Philips dedicated the printed text of *The Revengeful Queen* to the Duke of Ormond, declaring: "It is an old Observation that one Misfortune always attends another. I have sufficiently experimented it; and I may as justly say the same thing of my folly, in the Conduct of my Life, and in what relates to this Play. It was folly in me to Write at all, greater to Write no better, and chiefly to Print what I have Writ." He goes on to flatter Ormond

9. *Dictionary of National Biography,* ed. Sidney Lee, XV (London, 1909), 1068.
10. *The London Stage 1660–1800, Part I : 1660–1700,* ed. William Van Lennep (Carbondale : Southern Illinois University Press, 1965), p. 496. Another play, *Alcamenes and Menalippa,* is sometimes attributed to Philips. For example, Gertrude L. Woodward and James G. Mc Manaway, *A Check List of English Plays 1641–1700* (Chicago : The Newberry Library, 1945), p. 100. The date is given as 1668. But in his dedication to *The Revengeful Queen* Philips states the latter to be his first play.
11. *The Revengeful Queen: A Tragedy . . .* Written by William Philips, Esq; (London, 1698), Prologue, lines 13–18.

with the suggestion that he might shield Philips and his
play from their enemies. "And indeed, I may say it is
natural in me, to claim this from you; because your Family
have vouchsafed to be the Patrons of mine for several
Generations." Further elaboration of this patronage would
be of some interest; one wonders what form it can have
taken. In any event, Philips stood in need of a patron for
this play, since it was not a success on stage.

In his monumental survey of Restoration drama, Robert
Hume speaks of *The Revengeful Queen* as if it were an
expression of the current taste for "blood-bath" drama.[12]
This implies a play which met the demands of its audiences.
But it is quite clear that *The Revengeful Queen*, which is
an historical tragedy set in Gothic Italy, pleased not the
million. Indeed Philips himself, speaking of the eponymous
queen and her husband, declared in the dedication that
"the Characters of Alboino and Rosamund are not agreeable to the present Taste of the Town." He claimed credit,
however, for "the truth of the story" as taken from
Machiavelli's *The Florentine History*. There was criticism,
apparently, over the resemblance of Philips's play to
Davenant's *The Tragedy of Albovine, King of the Lom-
bards* (1629), and Philips was forced to deny any impu-
tation of plagiarism. He insisted that he was ignorant of
Davenant's play: "I knew it not before, nor have I yet
seen it: It was very unhappy for me to happen on the
same Subject with so Ingenious a Person." In Philips's
defence, it can be said that his tragedy is closer to
Machiavelli's account than is Davenant's.

Philips's next play was a new departure for him. It was
a comedy of manners, written, as he states in the Epistle
Dedicatory, expressly "for our *Irish* Stage." It is clear that

12. Robert D. Hume, *The Development of English Drama in
the Late Seventeenth Century* (Oxford : Clarendon Press,
1976), pp. 448–9.

Philips and the dedicatee, William O'Brien, Third Earl of Inchiquin, had had prior discussion over the proper purpose of comedy. O'Brien, it seems, had strong views on drama "Encouraging Virtue, and Exposing Vice" and he wanted the stage "Reform'd from the Corruption of Manners" so that "Decency, Modesty, and Good Breeding" should be installed there. The Epistle Dedicatory makes plain that *St Stephen's Green* was written in compliance with these sentiments.

If he is to be believed, Dubliners gave Philips nothing but encouragement with his play, for he says in the Epistle Dedicatory: "They have sufficiently evidenced how Inclinable they are to Encourage Wit and Poetry, by being so Favourable and so Generous to my weak Attempts on both." In spite of this remark, and Philips's reference to "the Criticks", the *Biographia Dramatica* and some of the commentators who have followed it declare that *St Stephen's Green* was never acted. The authors of *Biographia Dramatica*, however, confessed that they had never seen the text.[13] Had they looked no further than the title page they would have seen the description, "as it is Acted at / The Theatre-Royal." It may also be noted here that Richard Leveridge, who is known to have fled London for Ireland for the year 1699–1700,[14] is named as the arranger for the song in act five.

13. David Erskine Baker, Isaac Reid, and Stephen Jones, *Biographia Dramatica* (3 vols., London, 1812), III, 239. "This piece was never acted, nor have we ever seen it." J.W.C. also states that the play was "never acted", in "The Dramatic Writers of Ireland—No. II", *Dublin University Magazine*, XLV (Jan–June 1855), 174.
14. *The London Stage 1660–1800, Part I*, p. 521. The source is a letter from John Vanbrugh to the Earl of Manchester, 25 December 1699: "Liveridge is in Ireland, he Owes so much money he dare not come over, so for want of him we han't had one Opera play'd this Winter."

Whatever the reception which greeted *St Stephen's Green* on its first production during the season 1699–1700, it apparently was not enough to encourage Philips to a sequel. Indeed, his next play was not staged until 1722, and not in Dublin but in Lincoln's Inn Fields, London. (His last play was to be staged in that same theatre two years later.) A question mark, therefore, hangs over the whole relationship of Philips with the Dublin stage. It is proper, at this point, to ask what motivated him to write for the Theatre Royal in Smock Alley since it was not usual for an ambitious writer to occupy himself with the Dublin stage. George Farquhar, who, as a native of Derry, was virtually Philips's next-door neighbour, is a typical case. Having acted at Smock Alley from about 1696 to 1698 Farquhar went to London to pursue his career as a writer : *Love and a Bottle* was staged at Drury Lane in 1698 and was followed by *The Constant Couple* (1699) and later *The Recruiting Officer* and *The Beaux' Stratagem*. These plays became popular in Dublin only after they had proved successful in London. William Congreve, likewise, moved to London in the early sixteen nineties as soon as he graduated from Trinity College. In contrast, Philips was showing himself to be particularly patriotic by writing for the Dublin theatre. In the Epistle Dedicatory, indeed, he expresses the wish that other writers, of a "happier Genius", might be encouraged by his own "Success". As William Smith Clark has commented, Philips's Epistle Dedicatory is "the earliest admission by a native author of a concern for a self-contained and distinctive theatre in Ireland." [15] As will be made clear in the section below which explores the text in detail, *St Stephen's Green* was written with some patriotic feeling.

It is, no doubt, puzzling why there should have been

15. William Smith Clark, *The Early Irish Stage The Beginnings to 1720* (Oxford : Clarendon Press, 1955), p. 117.

such a long interval between *St Stephen's Green*, published
in 1700, and Philips's next play, *Hibernia Freed*, which
appeared in 1722. It would seem that Philips published
nothing in the interim. If one wants to find a possible
reason for this long silence, one must speculate, using rather
flimsy evidence. As early as 1697, Philips had been described as 'Captain'; if, therefore, he was a military man
whose writing took second place to his career as a soldier,
a possible explanation becomes available for his lack of
composition during the first two decades of the eighteenth
century. He may well have been on the continent during
the wars with France, for example. There is, in fact, a
Captain William Philips recorded in *English Army Lists*
attached to a regiment of foot under the Irish nobleman,
Lord Ikerrin, between 1702 and 1706. In the "Calendar
of State Papers/British Departmental Correspondence 1683
to 1714" in the Public Record Office of Ireland there is
mention of a Captain Philips's resignation from Brudenall's
regiment in August 1703; through 1705 he is mentioned
in connection with money due and a position sought, and
in 1706 he has his own company in a regiment serving in
Spain. Lord Ikerrin's regiment was in Spain at this time.
Philips probably saw action in Flanders also. His last play,
Belisarius, is dedicated to General Webb, of whom Philips
speaks with affection: "I persuade my self, I have the
Honour to be so well known to You, that You will not
imagine I have the common Aim of Dedications in view.
Allow me however to assure You, That I have no other
End in this, but to boast of some Share in Your Friend-
ship." [16] In the dedication, Philips draws a parallel between
the Gothic general Belisarius and the English general

16. *Belisarius. A Tragedy* . . . Written by William Philips, Esq;
(London, 1724). This quotation, and the one following, come
from the "Dedication", A4.

Webb. The language suggests that Philips was a fellow
soldier :

> A Reflection on this Subject naturally introduces to
> one's Thoughts the important and glorious Victory
> You obtain'd at *Winnendale*; where, and in a cham-
> pion Country, the Enemy had eight and twenty
> thousand Men, and they veteran Troops, of which
> there were sixty Squadrons of Horse; and your whole
> Force consisted but of six thousand, including but one
> Squadron; they posses'd of sixty Cannon, and You
> had not one. . . . A Victory, which gave Preservation
> to the whole Confederate Army, added Glory to Your
> Country, and confers on You immortal Reputation,
> tho' Your intrepid Behaviour at *Namure*, *Blenheim*,
> *Tanniers* and other Places was in Oblivion. . . . Were
> I sollicitous about the Sale of this Play, I would here
> attempt to describe so signal an Action. An exact and
> faithful Account of that wou'd be an universal Induce-
> ment to buy, and the Dedication would then be an
> Attonement for my Poetry. But I hope that will be
> executed by some more skilful Hand, nor wou'd I rob
> the History of this Age of one of the noblest Incidents
> in it.

But even soldiers have to have a home to come to, and
Dublin may have continued as Philips's home during the
first decade of the eighteenth century. Parish records indicate the birth of a girl, Sarah, to William Phillips [*sic*]
on 14 July 1700[17]; and the birth of a boy, George, to
William and Jane Philips on 28 December 1711.[18] Philips

17. *The Registers of S. Catherine, Dublin, 1636–1715*, ed.
Herbert Wood (Exeter and London : William Pollard, 1908),
p. 129.
18. *The Register of St. Nicholas Without, Dublin, 1694–1739*,
ed. James Mills (Exeter : William Pollard, 1912), p. 36.

may have succeeded his father as a member of the Irish Parliament. The *Journals of the House of Commons* record a William Philips as member in 1707 and 1711; this man, apparently, was also known as 'Captain' Philips. On 18 October 1707 Robert Johnson, Baron of the Exchequer, wrote to the Duke of Ormond about a fracas in the House of Commons, during some elections, when Lady Donegal was, it seems, ejected from the House. "For one Mr. Philips, a member who can sometimes turn fables into verses and being a relation of the Donegal family was incensed to see the judge either take or be given a privilege which the Countess was refused, went up to the gallery, where he was, and bid the judge remove, which he seeming not to mind, he told the judge he must be gone out, for that place was not a place for him, upon which the other told the captain he wanted manners. These being words that naturally put captains into a flame and make them forget their respects to the furs and ermine, the captain brustled up to him and told him he was a villain and that he despised him and all that belonged to him." [19] The row was, however, quelled by "some charitable person".

William Philips's name does not appear in records relating to the Irish Parliament later than October 1712.[20] It is possible that Philips ended his political career with the death of Queen Anne; that is, if he and the Captain Philips mentioned above are one and the same man. The dedication to *Belisarius* reveals open sympathy with the fallen general Webb, who was accused of Jacobite interests. It may be supposed that Philips went to London after the

---

19. *Historical Manuscripts Commission. Calendar of the Manuscripts of the Marquess of Ormonde, K.P.* New Series, VIII (London, 1920), 313. I am indebted to Mr Donal Looney, National Library of Ireland, for this reference.
20. *Calendar of Ancient Records of Dublin*, ed. John T. Gilbert, VI (Dublin, 1896), 466.

change of government. He was obviously a member of an Irish set in London by the time he brought out *Hibernia Freed* in February 1722. One critic remarked: "I never knew a Play so Clapped . . . till a Friend put me in Mind that half the Audience were *Wild Irish*." [21]

Hibernia Freed was dedicated to Henry O'Brien, eighth Earl of Thomond. The dedication makes clear that Philips retained a patriotic attitude, even if he was now writing for the London stage: "Love of my Country induced me to lay the Scene of a Play there." [22] His play deals with the Danish occupation of Ireland, and the resistance of O'Brien, "Monarch of *Ireland*". Philips is celebrating his patron's noble ancestor, "for what is so noble as to free ones Country from Tyranny and Invasion?" The fervour of this dedication defines Philips as a nationalist. The passing of the Sixth of George the First (the Declaratory Act) in March 1720, which severely curtailed the freedom of Ireland, may have incensed Philips as it incensed his countryman Jonathan Swift. At this time it was common for drama to allegorize political situations, and *Hibernia Freed* can readily be seen as a veiled presentation of Ireland's woes.

Viewed dispassionately, *Hibernia Freed* may be, as Genest said long ago, "a dull Tragedy with little or no incident till the 5th act." [23] The quality of the history, also, leaves something to be desired, since Turgesius and Brian Boru are made contemporaneous and a love story is fabricated to add romantic interest. Still, the play is an interesting attempt, for Irish history was even less well known

21. *The London Stage 1660–1800, Part 2: 1700–1729*, ed. Emmett L. Avery (2 vols., Carbondale: Southern Illinois University Press, 1960), p. clxiv.
22. *Hibernia Freed. A Tragedy* . . . (London, 1722), "Dedication". There was also a Dublin printing of this play in 1722.
23. John Genest, *Some Account of the English Stage* (10 vols., Bath, 1832), III, 80.

in London then than it is now. Philips was aware that he
was asking audiences to listen. He was not giving them the
usual round of distractions. In his Prologue he is almost
apologetic about this: *"Fain wou'd we please and common
Arts avoid, / For soon with Repitition you are cloy'd."*
One stout soul, probably an Irishman, wrote in the *Daily
Journal* the day *before* the first performance: "The Play
for Diction, and fine Sentiments is not inferiour to any
Dramatick Piece that has appear'd on either Stage these
24 Years." [24] But this is a partisan view. *Hibernia Freed*
does not really rank with Addison's *Cato*.

The play opens on *"The Hill of* Tarah", where O'Brien
listens mournfully to the harp-playing of his bard Eugenius.
When he speaks it is to bewail at considerable length
Ireland's misfortunes. This must be the first time the *ochone*
is heard in Anglo-Irish drama:

> Fertile *Hibernia*! Hospitable Land!
> Is not allow'd to feed her Native Sons,
> In vain they toil, and a-mid Plenty starve.
> The lazy *Dane* grows wanton with our Stores,
> Urges our Labour, and derides our Wants.
> *Hibernia*! Seat of Learning! School of Science!
> How waste! How wild dost thou already seem!
> Thy Houses, Schools, thy Cities ransack'd, burnt!
> Virgins are torn from the fond Parent's Arms,
> And offer'd up t'appease their fancy'd Gods;
> Or worse, must yield to gratify the *Dane*.   (p. 9)

News is brought of a successful uprising in Ulster, led by
O'Neil [*sic*], who enters in act two. He is at least as
interested in O'Brien's daughter, Sabina, as in driving out
the Danes; since Turgesius is drawn also to Sabina the
central conflict is swiftly set up. Sabina has no time for
love, in the present circumstances:

24. Quoted in *The London Stage 1660–1800, Part 2,* p. xciv.

Look round and see what Desolation reigns.
My King, my Father robb'd of native Right.
Empire is lost and Liberty is fled.
Murder and Rapine waste our peaceful Land :
And can I bear unmov'd my Country's Wrongs?
And thus afflicted can I hear of Love? (p. 34)

Might, however, is right in Turgesius's eyes, and he commands O'Brien to send Sabina to his bed, accompanied by fourteen maids for his friends, "My Partners in the Toyls of War" (p. 46). The scene then changes to the Danish camp, and the women are led in, muffled in long black veils. At the opportune moment the 'women' unveil to reveal O'Neil and his men. The cowardly enemy takes flight once Turgesius is defeated and the play ends with a prophecy from Eugenius about Ireland's glory under English rule. This speech is a glowing tribute to "this other Eden", and rather cuts across the idea of colonial nationalism (to borrow the phrase from J. G. Simms) suggested by the preceding play. Perhaps it was meant to appease the Lord Chamberlain. Or it may contain a naïve hope on Philips's part that the English conquest would lead to unity :

They shall succeed, invited to our Aid,
And mix their Blood with ours; one People grow,
Polish our Manners, and improve our Minds. (p. 61)

One wonders, however, what significance attaches to the omission of Eugenius—the spokesman for this colonial view of Irish history—from the production revived for St. Patrick's day, 1722.[25]

Hibernia Freed was staged once in Dublin in 1722, either before or after the London production.[26] In all, the

25. Ibid., p. 669.
26. *Hibernia Freed* is listed for one performance in 1722, by Rev. S. C. Hughes, *The Pre-Victorian Drama in Dublin* (Dublin : Hodges, Figgis, 1904), p. 61.

play had seven performances at the Lincoln's Inn Fields theatre, which was a reasonable run. It meant that the author got his two "benefit" nights (February 17 and 22) amounting to almost one hundred and eighty pounds.[27] The play was well cast, with Boheme as O'Brien and James Quin as Turgesius. Quin had begun his acting career at Smock Alley, and had made his mark in London in 1716 when he played Bajazet in Rowe's *Tamerlane*. He was to become the greatest actor of his age, renowned for his classical, declamatory style. Others in the cast included Lacy Ryan (O'Neil), who had played Marcus in the first production of *Cato* in 1713. Thomas Walker played Erric, confidant to Turgesius; he was to play Macheath in the first production of *The Beggar's Opera* in 1728, after which the applause proved "fatal to him" and he took to drink.[28] Mrs. Bullock, a natural daughter of Robert Wilks, played Agnes, daughter of Herimon, and Charles Hulet played Herimon, an Irish chief. Hulet had already played one season at Smock Alley, so that Philips may be said to have assembled an Irish cast for his play. Hulet had a good voice (and was said later to have surpassed Walker as Macheath), but he took a certain pride in its volume, "for he had an odd Custom of stealing unperceiv'd upon a Person and with a *Hem!* in his Ear deafen him for some time",[29] a practice which apparently brought about his death from a burst blood vessel.

Many of this same cast appeared also in Philips's last play, *Belisarius*, staged at the same theatre on 14 April 1724. It ran for six nights and was revived for two more performances within a year.[30] It was not, however, well

27. *The London Stage 1660–1800, Part 2*, p. 664.
28. W. R. Chetwood, *A General History of the Stage; (More Particularly the Irish Theatre)* (Dublin, 1749), p. 250.
29. Ibid., p. 175.
30. *The London Stage 1660–1800, Part 2*, pp. 770, 771, 796, 807.

supported. (Philips's "benefit" receipts totalled less than one hundred and twenty-five pounds.) The play deserved better, as at least one spectator was aware: "But how contemptible an Opinion must the next Generation have of this Age, if it should be known amongst them; that the first Night this Tragedy appear'd upon the Stage, it did not bring half a House, because it happen'd to be upon a Masquerade Night." [31] Philips was aiming high, attempting to keep blank verse tragedy alive at a bad time. *"Can we then please in so polite an Age? / When Sense and Learning only fly the Stage"* he asks in the Prologue. Aware of the odds, he is willing to try:

> *The following Scenes he offers to your View,*
> *Nor dares your Censure, nor can meanly sue.*
> *But hope not Towns besieg'd, and Battles fought,*
> *And in one Play ten diff'rent Stories brought.*
> *And sure the Stage shou'd still be chaste and clean,*
> *From Deeds of Horror, and from Words obscene. . . .*
> *Happy the Man! who shall reform the Stage,*
> *Improve our Judgment, and refine the Age.*[32]

Philips is too modest to be radical here: *"To Rules you dictate, chearful we comply,"* he wrote. But he did break with convention enough to have a serious epilogue, which Allardyce Nicoll sees as a rare attempt to recapture "some of the tragic spirit" at this time almost lost to the English stage.[33]

31. Ibid., p. 770. The quotation is from the *Weekly Journal or Saturday's Post*, 18 April 1722. Was it entirely coincidental that Philips should speak in the Epilogue of the *"dreaded Masquerade"*?
32. *Belisarius. A Tragedy . . .* (London, 1724), Prologue, lines 15–26.
33. Allardyce Nicoll, *A History of English Drama 1660–1900,* II (Cambridge: University Press, 1969), 64.

The story of Belisarius, the victorious Gothic soldier who ended up blind and outcast under the emperor Justinian, has been made familiar to modern readers through the version by Robert Graves (*Count Belisarius*). Philips, while restricted by the formal and contrived style of the early eighteenth century, was able to give considerable grandeur and pathos to the story. In particular, the scene where the blinded Belisarius is brought in contact with his unsuspecting lover, Almira, is admirably managed. Allardyce Nicoll says it "rises to a height rare in the early eighteenth century".[34] Although not a theatrical success, *Belisarius* made an impression: the phrase to "give a penny to Belisarius" seems to have become proverbial.[35] A second edition of the play appeared in 1758, with an introduction supplying a resumé of Belisarius' historical career.

By that time Philips was long dead. No details have come to light concerning his career between the production of *Belisarius* in 1724 and his death on 12 December 1734. To complicate matters, there was another Captain Philips who was an author living in London about 1720. He too had an interest in Irish affairs. He was attaché to Sir Thomas Hanmer, Speaker of the House of Commons. One finds reference to him in the "Calendar of State Papers / British Departmental Correspondence" (P.R.O.I.) as early as 1706/7. He was, it seems, interested in plays, for he writes at one point (March 1707) that Farquhar's last play was about to be staged in London, and that he hoped it would live even if its author was dead. This Philips was known to Swift, and is mentioned in Swift's *Correspondence*.[36] In 1721 he brought out *The Romance of the Rose*,

34. Ibid., p. 107.
35. According to John Genest, *Some Account of the English Stage*, III, 146–7.
36. *Correspondence of Jonathan Swift*, ed. F. Elrington Ball

imitated from Chaucer. It was published anonymously, but the copy presented to Worcester College Library, Oxford, ascribes it to Captain Philips. It contains two passages laudatory of Hanmer, so the ascription is likely to be correct. Coincidentally, the poem was published by Jonah Bowyer, who published *Hibernia Freed* in 1722, so that it seems almost impossible that the two Captain Philipses did not know each other. There is no doubt whatever, though, who was the author of the plays, since each of the published texts has a dedication signed "Will. Philips" and all but one of the four title pages carry the name "William Philips". The exception is *Hibernia Freed*.

In the end, then, a certain amount of mystery surrounds the life and career of William Philips. As an Irish writer who wrote in the "age of Swift" he was a minor figure, but perhaps even Lilliputians have a place in the scheme of things.

II   THE IRISH THEATRE IN THE LATE
       SEVENTEENTH CENTURY

John Ogilby, the man who had opened the first professional theatre in Dublin in 1637, built a new theatre immediately following the Restoration of Charles II. It was the first Restoration theatre to be built in these islands, a theatre with a royal patent. The site was in Smock Alley, at the rere of the Lower Blind Quay, where the Church of SS. Michael and John stands to-day.

Early in December 1662 the poet Katherine Philips wrote from Dublin to a friend: "We have Plays here in

(6 vols., London, 1910–1914), II, 106, n. 1. Confusingly, the reference to Will. Phillips [*sic*] in a letter from Prior to Swift, 25 September 1718, seems to be to the playwright. See III, 14.

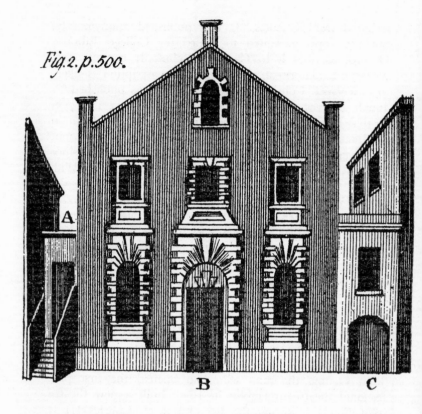

Fig.2.p.500.

Sketch of the second Smock Alley first published in *Gentleman's Magazine*, June 1789.

The key is : A. The upper gallery door of the theatre.
               B. The door to the boxes.
               C. The passage to the pit and the middle gallery.

the newest Mode, and not ill acted." [37] By the "newest Mode" was meant staging with changeable scenery and in a manner similar to but "much finer than D'AVENANT'S" theatre at Lisle's Tennis Court in London. It was probably a plain enough building, rectangular in shape. That the exterior was unprepossessing is suggested by the omission of the theatre from the pictorial details of Charles Brooking's map of Dublin in 1728; had it been among the beauties of the town it should certainly have been depicted. As to size, one theatre historian (Hughes[38]) says Smock Alley theatre measured 63 feet by 139 feet, while another (Clark[39]) estimates it to have been 55 feet by 110 feet. If Hughes is right Smock Alley was as big as Dorset Garden theatre, which it anticipated by nine years; if Clark is right Smock Alley was as big as the first Drury Lane, which it anticipated by one year. One might guess the capacity to have been about six hundred persons, perhaps one per-cent of Dublin's population in the latter part of the seventeenth century.

As is known from John Dunton's description of the theatre, to be quoted later, Smock Alley comprised the arrangement which was to become standard in theatres all through the British Isles. The auditorium was divided into pit, boxes and galleries, and the stage area lay half behind and half in front of a proscenium arch. (It is strange to think that the Abbey Theatre (1904) stayed within this basic, traditional structure as evolved in the Restoration and Georgian theatre.) It seems, however, that neither acoustics nor sightlines were of the very best in this pro-

37. Quoted La Tourette Stockwell, *Dublin Theatres and Theatre Customs (1637–1820)* (Kingsport, Tenn. : Kingsport Press, 1938; New York : Benjamin Blom, 1968), p. 27.
38. Rev. S. C. Hughes, *The Pre-Victorian Drama in Dublin*, p. 3. Cf. La Tourette Stockwell, *Dublin Theatres and Theatre Customs*, p. 311, n. 23.
39. William Smith Clark, *The Early Irish Stage*, p. 53.

scenium theatre.[40] Moreover, whether owing to an archi-
tectural flaw or, as some contemporaries insisted, because
of its devilish activities, Smock Alley was more than once
threatened with collapse. Indeed, the galleries did collapse
once during a performance in 1670, killing three or four
people and injuring several more, including the Lord
Lieutenant and one of his sons.[41] It seems more than unfair
of some historians doggedly to insist that the same thing
happened again in 1701; the theatre had troubles enough
as it was, since the wars of 1688–91 closed it completely.
The reopening after peace was declared on 23 March
1692, however, ushered in a new phase in the fortunes of
Smock Alley, and it is with this phase that we are now
concerned.

Smock Alley was at this time in the hands of Joseph
Ashbury, actor and manager. Ashbury had the gift of
attracting real talent to the theatre. His practice was to
make occasional forays into the London theatre and bring
back promising young actors and actresses. These he would
instruct and encourage in the art of acting until, inevitably,
they returned to London and (usually) carved their names
in the theatrical annals there. One such foray in 1694
added eight names to the Smock Alley company. Chief
among these was Robert Wilks, who was in fact returning
after a tentative sojourn in London. Wilks, who was born
in Dublin in 1670, was to become one of the stars of the
English stage. He began under Ashbury's direction in 1691,
playing Othello in a private performance. He became
infatuated with the stage and threw up his position as clerk
to Robert Southwell (Secretary of State for Ireland).[42] At

40. Robert Hitchcock, *An Historical View of the Irish Stage*
(2 vols., Dublin, 1788, 1794), I, 93–4.
41. La Tourette Stockwell, *Dublin Theatres and Theatre
Customs*, p. 33.
42. Colley Cibber, *An Apology for the Life of Mr. Colley
Cibber, Comedian* (Dublin, 1740), p. 136.

Smock Alley Wilks befriended George Farquhar and later starred in his plays. Another notable acquisition by Ashbury was Dick Estcourt, a famous mimic. Steele was to call him the best man in the world "for heightening the revel-gaiety of a company" with his infectious humour.[43] These two actors were joined a few years later (June 1698) by Barton Booth, an English schoolboy from Westminster who had run away to be a player. He too was destined for fame on the English stage. But he began in Dublin under layers of lampblack, playing Oroonoko. He did this so well, however, that Ashbury "rewarded him with a Present of Five Guineas",[44] and he won the Dubliners' affection. He stayed for two years. Others to arrive in 1698 included William Bowen and Thomas Griffith (both Irishmen), Joseph Trefusis and Miss Cross. The latter was a singer, a young beauty, then regarded as a second Nell Gwynn. All of this talent meant that Smock Alley had a company as strong as it ever was to be. It was particularly strong in comedy. One of the rare facts known about the repertory at this time is that the three comedies of George Etherege, *The Comical Revenge, She Would is She Could* and *The Man of Mode*, were staged in 1698 : the cast lists have survived.[45] Chetwood also mentions that Mrs Ashbury excelled as Margery Pinchwife in Wycherley's *The Country Wife*, and as she took leading roles in 1698–99 it seems likely that that comedy was staged then also. In other words, when *St Stephen's Green* was produced in 1699–1700 there was

43. Quoted by W. J. Lawrence, "New Light on the Old Dublin Stage", *The New Ireland Review*, XXVI (Nov. 1906), 162, n. 9.
44. W. R. Chetwood, *A General History of the Stage*, p. 92.
45. Ibid., pp. 53–55. Chetwood does not supply dates for these performances, but cross reference with *The London Stage 1660–1800*, Parts 1 and 2, shows that Chetwood's casts could only have been at Dublin in 1698. Cf. Clark, *The Early Irish Stage*, pp. 112–13.

available a company well skilled in Restoration comedy.
1698 also saw the visit to Dublin of the London bookseller John Dunton. He spent nine months in Dublin (from
Spring 1698), and his account in *The Dublin Scuffle* is
invaluable for the light it throws on Dublin social life. As
to the theatre, Dunton describes how he saw a playbill for
The Squire of Alsatia, a comedy by Thomas Shadwell first
staged at Drury Lane in 1688. Although he knew the play,
he was tempted to go along to the performance that afternoon. Almost every detail of Dunton's description of Smock
Alley and of the play is significant. He mentions the pur-
chasing of a ticket and entering the pit, greeting some ladies
of his acquaintance and calling to the *"China Orange
Wench"* for her wares. He was surprised by the interior :

> I found, Madam, the Dublin *Play-house* to be a place
> very contrary to its owners; for they on their out-sides
> make the best show : But this is *very ordinary in its
> outward appearance*, but looks much better on the
> inside, with its *Stage, Pit, Boxes, two Galleries, Lettices,*
> and *Musick Loft*; though I must confess, that even
> these, like other *false Beauties*, receive a Lustre from
> their Lamps and Candles.[46]

The lettices, incidentally, were boxes with windows, situated
over the stage doors; the music loft was over the proscenium, as in the well-known engraving by Dolle of *The
Empress of Morocco*, showing Dorset Garden Theatre
(1673). Dunton goes on to confess that he arrived dressed
more like a beau than a bookseller, powdered wig and all,
"tho' not so much to be seen, as to see the Follies of the
Age". The theatre was very crowded (a tribute to Ashbury's
management); indeed, Dunton reflected that no church he
had visited in Dublin was half so crowded. In spite of his

46. John Dunton, *The Dublin Scuffle* (London, 1699), pp.
339–40.

unease at the size of the crowd, Dunton enjoyed the play :
" 'Twas pretty to see the *Squire choused* out of so fair an
Estate with so very little *ready Rino*," he remarked, bor-
rowing the playwright's argot. He spent about four hours
in the theatre, which argues intervals, probably with music.
All in all (and Dunton names the actors and actresses also),
Smock Alley was found to be well up to London standard.

And what of the audience at Smock Alley at this time?
Would it be fair to imagine it unsophisticated, so starved
for entertainment that it would accept just about anything?
Dunton testifies that the audience was no different from
that attending a London theatre. Smock Alley, one must
recall, was reliant for patronage on high society, and
especially on the Lord Lieutenant and his circle. The
theatre was a fashionable resort, and, consequently, high
standards were expected : after all, this was a theatre *royal*,
the third in the kingdom. The cheapest seat, in the top
gallery, was one shilling, which was more than a peasant
or a workman could afford. Smock Alley was, perhaps,
élitist as well as colonial.

The quality of the patronage ensured that the theatre
was conservative and docile in the conduct of its affairs. In
1697 Joseph Ashbury was prosecuted and fined for swearing
on stage,[47] which shows that Dublin was more inhibited
than London at this time. This may explain the tone of
Philips's Epistle Dedicatory to *St Stephen's Green*, where
he is at such pains to assure his patron of the moral purity
of his play. Government influence in political rather than
moral terms was not a factor at this time; it came after

47. La Tourette Stockwell, *Dublin Theatres and Theatre
Customs*, pp. 39–41; William Smith Clark, *The Early Irish
Stage*, p. 105. Cf. Robert D. Hume, *The Development of
English Drama in the Late Seventeenth Century*, p. 434 :
"There are rumours of prosecutions of actors in 1699, but
our first hard evidence comes from 1701."

1700, when the theatre became a "semi-governmental institution".[48]

Apart from the nobility, the theatre was patronized by the wits and the ladies. The pit was, traditionally, the place where the wits or the intelligentsia sat. If Philips is to be believed, they could be quite a nuisance :

> *Hither such come to Censure, not to Hear,*
> *And whisper dull remarks in's Neighbour's Ear.*
> *Chat the whole Play, then Judgment give at Guess,*
> *And damn the Poet for the Actor's dress.*
> *Strut in the Pit, Survey the Gallery,*
> *In hopes to be lur'd up by some kind She.*
>
> (Prologue, *St Stephen's Green*)

Many of these beaux must have been students from Trinity College. In 1696 Archbishop King complained that the young men of Dublin were attending more to the playhouse than to their studies.[49] Women, of course, formed a most important part of the audience. John Dunton comments immediately on the ladies he met at Smock Alley; he had dressed like a beau because he knew they would be there. In Philips's play the two young girls confess to being frequent playgoers, and it would have been an accepted social venue, as it was later to be for Jane Austen's heroines at Bath. The ladies usually graced the boxes, but ladies of easier virtue sat in the gallery together with the other professional classes. Generally speaking, the Dublin audience could not be taken for granted : complaints about empty houses are a familiar theme in Prologues. The trick for playwright and manager was to win the audience's loyalty

48. W. J. Lawrence, "New Light on the Old Dublin Stage", p. 156.
49. John T. Gilbert, *A History of the City of Dublin* (3 vols., Dublin, 1861), II, 70.

as the actors were sometimes able to do. Robert Wilks, beginning on the London stage, said :

> I left a distant Isle too kind to me.
> Loaded with Favors I was forc'd away,
> 'Cause I wou'd not accept what I cou'd never pay.
> There I cou'd please, but there my Fame must end,
> For hither none must come to boast, but mend.[50]

The words were in fact by Farquhar. When Farquhar returned to Dublin to act in his own comedy *The Constant Couple* in 1704 he was so bad, apparently, that even his friends were embarrassed for him. Yet Farquhar made almost one hundred pounds on this occasion.[51] The audience could be relied upon not to savage its own.

No doubt, the best was yet to come. A new and finer building was erected on the site of the old Smock Alley in 1735, and Thomas Sheridan was to bring it to its period of greatest fame in the seventeen forties and fifties. Yet the early days had their achievements too, not least of which was in establishing firmly a theatrical tradition in Dublin. Jonathan Swift was no playgoer, but in 1720 (the year of the manager Ashbury's death) he could describe Smock Alley as "That Simple House [which] is the Fountain of all our Love, Wit, Dress, and Gallantry." [52]

---

50. George Farquhar, "An Epilogue, Spoken by Mr. Wilks", in *Love and Business: In a Collection of Occasionary Verse, and Epistolary Prose* (London, 1702), pp. 39–40.
51. La Tourette Stockwell, *Dublin Theatres and Theatre Customs*, p. 53.
52. Quoted by William Smith Clark, *The Early Irish Stage*, p. 176.

III   St. Stephen's-Green
AND THE DRAMA OF ITS TIME

St Stephen's Green is something of a Janus: it looks back-
ward to the traditions established by Restoration comedy
and it looks forward to the history of Irish drama in
English. With regard to the former, it is well to bear in
mind here the emphasis recently made by scholars on the
diversity which lies behind the blanket description, 'Restoration comedy'. It is no longer possible simply to describe
this kind of drama as comedy of manners, or comedy of
wit. Indeed, the notion that it is possible to find a definition
which will hold good for all comedies produced between
1660 and 1710 must be abandoned. It is not advantageous,
accordingly, to assess *St Stephen's Green* in the light of
formulations derived from a study of the plays of Dryden
or Etherege or Wycherley, plays written a quarter of a
century earlier. It makes more sense to relate the play to
its own decade, the sixteen nineties, and to the change in
taste which took place at that time. As Robert Hume has
pointed out, comedy altered in the sixteen nineties, the
older, "hard" comedy yielding to a more romantic, "humane" comedy.[53] It is as "humane" comedy, on the brink
of what was to become sentimental comedy in later decades,
that *St Stephen's Green* can properly be understood.

In some respects, *St Stephen's Green* contains no sur-
prises. We meet the two pairs of witty lovers customary in
the best known comedies of the Restoration period. We find
that love is balked by a *senex* figure, who must be defeated

53. Robert D. Hume, *The Development of English Drama in
the Late Seventeenth Century*, pp. 143, 435. On the necessity
to see Restoration comedy as diverse, see also A. H. Scouten,
"Plays and Playwrights", in *The 'Revels' History of Drama
in English, Volume V 1660–1750* (London : Methuen, 1976),
p. 162.

before Jack has his Jill. We find a fop in Vainly, the affected dandy of Parisian tastes familiar from the prototypal Sir Fopling Flutter in *The Man of Mode* (1676). And we find abundance of witty repartee and social commentary, usual to London comedies after 1660. Because it conforms to such obvious elements Philips's play is to an extent conventional.

What is notable about the play, however, is its coherently moral design. It is not merely a matter of a tag line here or there, paying lipservice to virtue; the "right" way for man to live is the premise on which the whole play is based.[54] It is usual to point to *Love's Last Shift* (1696) as a turning point in Restoration drama. For four acts of Cibber's play the rake-hero, Loveless, disports himself as a Restoration libertine and then in the fifth act he is suddenly reformed. For the first time, conscience enters comedy as a motivating factor, and the hero is persuaded to recognize the force of virtue and its attractions. It is usual to see sentimental comedy as just around the corner, where the exemplary hero of Steele's *The Conscious Lovers* is waiting. The significant thing about Philips's play is that he does not use the sudden reform of his hero. His lovers are exemplary from the start.

It might be argued that Philips distinguishes between his two heroes, making Freelove considerably more moral. He is called "a Man of Sincerity" (II.i.442), and "the Sex's Knight Errant" (II.i.243-4). Less flatteringly, his friend calls him a "Downright Damn'd, Sober, Dull, Virtuous Fellow" (I.i.122-3). It must be realized, however, that the Freelove we see is a new man, reformed through

54. Cf. Norman N. Holland, *The First Modern Comedies, The Significance of Etherege, Wycherley and Congreve* (Bloomington and London : Indiana University Press, 1959). It can be said that by Philips's time the implicit moral theme of Restoration comedy had become explicit.

his love for Aemilia. Bellmine says to him : "I have known
the time, when you wou'd no more allow Virtue in
Womankind, than Honesty in a Jesuit" (I.i.150–1). Bellmine is more typical of the libertine, regarding the idea of
marriage as hateful, a "Precipice" (IV.i.128). "I dread it
as much as our Farmers do the Wool-Bill," he remarks
with a topical allusion (I.i.126–7). Refreshing as Bellmine
is, with a spontaneous response to womankind, he never
seriously challenges the moral code. He accepts the arrange-
ments made by society : " 'Tis a hard Case that we must
submit to the thing we Hate, before we can have the
Woman we Love" (I.i.142–3). Philips finds an outlet for
Bellmine's "wild civility",[55] however, in using it to ensnare
and expose Lady Volant. It is tamed and put to good use.

Because the men are already either reformed or on the
brink of reform the roles of the two girls are rather slight.
Apart from the incident of the masks, whereby they play
with the sincerity of their menfolk, the girls are passive
figures. They wait upon the whim (or libido) of Sir Francis
Feignyouth. Although they have little part in the action,
beyond the inspirational one implicit in their ideal status,
they are lively enough creations. It is hard not to believe
that Philips was borrowing from Etherege's *She Would if
She Could* here, although Gatty and Ariana are probably
more witty. Still, Marina has her moments. Under cover
of a mask she taunts Bellmine in the established manner :

> *Marina.* Poor Gentleman ! he has ran himself clear
> out of Breath by Protesting his Passion for me.

55. The theme of a praiseworthy book by Virginia Ogden
Birdsall, *Wild Civility The English Comic Spirit on the
Restoration Stage* (Bloomington and London : Indiana Uni-
versity Press, 1970). For treatment of the libertine and libertin-
ism, see Dale Underwood, *Etherege and the Seventeenth-
Century Comedy of Manners* (New Haven : Yale University
Press, 1957), chapter 2.

Bellmine. Who I, Madam? alas, I have said nothing yet; why Madam, if I do not admire your Wit, your Shape, your Mien, the colour of your Hair, your Fancy in your Dress, more than——

Marina. Have a Care what you say, Sir; pray let your Simile be short, for I fancy you are so very Fickle, that before you have made an end of it, your mind may change.

(I.i.299–307)

Aemilia, like Freelove, is a new type. She seems always to be either going to or coming from church. One pictures her as clasping a prayer book and wearing a black veil. In contrast to Marina she often seems demure ("No, that will not be so proper"—IV.i.392). She can display anger, however, at the belief that Freelove mistook her for a "mask" or whore, and this outburst animates her doll-like nature (II.i.496–533). Inasmuch as she is acting a part throughout, that of a poor relation, it is possible to see in the role aspects not at first sight forthcoming.

Some of the other characters are equally conventional. Trickwell, Freelove's servant, is the usual clever rogue, useful in furthering the intrigue and indispensable at the denouement. Making him the husband of Lady Volant may strain credulity but it winds up the plot neatly. Timothy Tellpenny is similarly functional, but at least he is physically memorable, with "that bloated Belly, and those bladder Cheeks, that Crimson Hue, and those huge Pillars which support thee" (IV.i.8–9). Philips probably wrote the part with a specific actor in mind. (Indeed, he would certainly have been limited to the cast available.) Wormwood, the town grouch, is perhaps the weakest character in the play. Perhaps Philips felt that the type, the malcontent, was worn out, and he pressed him into service in the plot, making him work as well as rail. It is out of character for Wormwood to advise Bellmine to break up the match between Sir Francis and Lady Volant, as the plot requires, though he defends himself at the time: " 'twill Gratifie my ill Nature, that thou shou'dst not follow good Counsel" (II.i.227–8). A mark of Philips's craftsmanship is that he makes these minor characters conscious of their roles, conscious of the "decorum" of comedy. If this makes them artificial it also calls upon the audience to participate in the game.

The triumph of the play, however, lies in the depiction of both Sir Francis Feignyouth and Lady Volant. Neither is entirely original. Sir Francis bears resemblance to Sir Sampson Legend in Congreve's *Love for Love* (1695), and Lady Volant is reminiscent of Lady Cockwood in Etherege's *She Would if She Could* (1668). Resemblances and echoes are inevitable, such is the familial nature of the drama of the time. But Philips is able to give sufficient stamp to both of his creations to bring them alive in their own right. Sir Francis is a role full of meat for the actor. He is ridiculous in his superannuated libertinism, but there is such gusto in his sensuality that he wins our affection. He operates at an energy level far in excess of the young men, which has the effect of making virtue seem pale by his side. For example, he deplores Bellmine's cautious realism over a lady's fortune: "Why, when I was a young Fellow, I never consider'd any thing but how to get a Mistress, and then how to get rid of her" (II.i.316–8). He chastizes the young men for not recognizing their own true loves behind masks, and in appreciating the qualities of these ladies (his own daughter and niece) he grows positively lecherous: "Talk of Portions! Look on 'em I say; there's a Motion, there's an Air, there's an Air: See, see, how firm they tread, hah? and then see their Hips, how they jut, how they rowl. Go, get ye gone, ye lazy Fellows, get ye gone. Ods me, don't stand staring after them, but follow them" (II.i.335–9). And when they exit he muses. "These young Fellows now adays are perfectly of the Womens temper, must be forc'd to do what they Languish for, or they keep themselves so low, they must take time to be rais'd; I believe I am brisker than any of them—How the Jades have fir'd me. Wou'd I cou'd meet with any thing that were not my own Flesh and Blood now" (II.i.343–8). Philips has made the older generation libidinous, the younger restrained, which is to invert the pattern of earlier Restoration comedy. Of course, the action ultimately validates the rightness of the restrained way: the plot is a trick to catch the old one, to shame him into an awareness of his folly. But in bringing about this worthy end Philips gives Sir Francis considerable line. He swallows the bait laid for him, an assignation with his own intended bride, regretting only the colour of her eyes, "only her Eyes, I cou'd wish her Eyes were Black" he keeps repeating (IV.i.210 ff.). His use of the regretful refrain in this passage is irresistible. At other times he is blunt and bluff in a comical manner, usually using repetition as part of his style. To Bellmine, "Phoo, trust to my Fatherly Love Boy, trust to that" (II.i.328). To Trickwell: "Heark ye Friend, if you wou'd have me believe you are in earnest, speak sense, speak sense d'ye see, and don't prate to me of Empires, and *Don Cupids*, and Darts, and such stuff, but tell me plainly, and in short, what it is you wou'd be at" (IV.i.157–61). Nor is he a disappointment when the revelation finally comes of the fool he has made of himself in marrying Lady Volant. He suffers as grandly as O'Casey's Captain Boyle was later to suffer. "I'm a dead Man, I'm stone dead!" (V.ii.146–7). He has to sit down to do justice to his grief: "What had I to do with a Wife, what had I to do with a Wife! Had I not Ease enough, had I not Freedom enough, had I not Wealth enough! I had every thing but Wit enough.—Oh! I am a Jest to the World, a Scandal to my Name, a Curse to my Family, and a Hell to my self" (V.ii.169–73). The delight in language here is unmistakable. This operatic grief slips momentarily into the bathos of financial realism, with an allusion to the confiscations of the late 1690s: "Had she Virtue, that were some atonement for her Poverty. Or had she been a Miss to some Favorite, and beg'd an Estate of Forfeited Lands, that had been some Comfort. But to be a Strumpet, and a poor Strumpet!" (V.ii.175–9). This is comedy of some edge, and given good acting it could hardly fail on stage.

Lady Volant's role has comparable riches, if it be accepted that its melodramatic content offers opportunities for bravura acting. She is really three types in one: the prattler, causing mischief by her wagging tongue; the hypocrite, veiling a sensual nature with protestations of primness and honour; and the opportunist, on the make for a fortune. Bellmine may say, "what a bottomless sink of Malice is her Breast" (I.i.428), but she hardly achieves any great depths of evil. The main thing about her is that she is an actress, adjusting her performance to whomever she is playing the scene: catty with Vainly, matronly with Marina and Aemilia, coy with Sir Francis, and sexy with Bellmine. Comedy arises when several of these parties are present together, and she is torn between one role and another. Here she plays like a *bad* actress. A good example is where she receives visitors in act three. She rebukes Sir Francis for his epicurean anticipations of the love feast: "Sir *Francis*, I have all the Respect and Friendship for you, that a Man of your Excellent Parts can require with Modesty, but I must desire you not to talk so loosly before me. Marriage is a sacred thing, Sir *Francis*, a very sacred thing; yet it is a thing, Sir *Francis*, that may be abus'd, and may be perverted to raise indecent and unruly Cogitations" (III.i.302–7). Repetition of his name, like a spell, shows how Lady Volant is playing with Sir Francis. Soon after this she is flirting with Bellmine in altogether a different language. He suggests an assignation on St Stephen's Green. She replies: "Oh me Sir, what wou'd the World say! or what I value more, what wou'd you think?"

(III.i.370–1). Bellmine is a total stranger to her, yet she values his opinion "more" than that of "the world"; this is a total contradiction of the morality she preaches to Sir Francis and also to the two young girls. She communicates, as it were, by italics, leaving the listener to gather her real meaning if he wishes. In this scene her many faces are exposed in quick succession. If this is rather crudely done (with Bellmine and Freelove unnecessarily underlining her guile) the same cannot be said of the assignation scene itself. Here Lady Volant shows what an actress she can be. Sir Francis arrives on St Stephen's Green muffled in a cloak, hoping to be mistaken for Bellmine, in an assignation with a nonexistent Siren. Lady Volant arrives masked, expecting to meet Bellmine. Very soon, each perceives who the other really is, but it is Lady Volant who takes charge of the situation. She unmasks with a flourish and acts the outraged innocent: "Ungrateful Worthless Fellow!" (V.i. 34). In a (feigned) double take she then sees that she is addressing Sir Francis and turns the heat on him. Quickly she gains the advantage: "is this like a Man of Honour? this the Behaviour I hop'd for from the worthy Sir *Francis*! I am ruin'd, undone, betray'd; what will become of me?" (V.i.68–70). And with Swiftian resolve she quits humankind: "No, I will never hearken to Man more. I will retire from the World, and leave my Wealth to erect Hospitals to maintain Mad men and Fools" (72–4). She has just about carried off the performance when Bellmine and Freelove enter, expecting to find an enlightened Sir Francis. Her job is to get clear now as soon as possible, and this she achieves with the threat of a fainting fit. This, undoubtedly, is Lady Volant's finest hour, and she pays for it later in the exposure scene. Even there, however, she shows a certain amount of aplomb, as after Wormwood reveals that her creditors would seize Sir Francis's plate unless he paid up: "What have you to answer to this?"—
—"That if you think the Plate worth Redeeming, you had

best send the Money" (V.ii.85–8). Doubtless, Lady Volant is reduced to a hissing villain in the end, a sort of Wilde cat, but well before that she establishes herself as a character with style.

The characterization, generally speaking, is of the 'humours' variety made popular by Thomas Shadwell (a great admirer of Ben Jonson). Indeed, Lady Volant has something in common with Mrs Termagant in *The Squire of Alsatia*, which had been such a success at Smock Alley a year or so earlier. There is, perhaps, a reference to that play in Sir Francis's remark, "I abhor a Termagant; I hate a Mistress that a Man must go to Cuffs with" (IV.i.208–9). But Etherege as well as Shadwell has influenced the characterization. Since Etherege's three comedies were staged at Smock Alley in 1698[56] it seems likely that Philips deliberately made use of popular material (Etherege's plays were also revived on the London stage in the sixteen nineties[57]). The two pairs of lovers are modelled on Etherege's in *She Would if She Could*, and Lady Volant recalls Lady Cockwood, who is also a consummate actress. The differences in Philips's treatment of Etherege's models reflect Philips's response to a greater interest in "poetic justice" in the sixteen nineties. In Etherege's play, for example, Lady Cockwood is never found out by her husband : overt moral purpose was not part of the design of Etherege's comedy as it was of Philips's.

56. W. R. Chetwood, *A General History of the Stage*, pp. 53–55. See above, n. 45.
57. *The London Stage 1660–1800, Part 1*, pp. 413, 466, 503. *She Would if She Could* was reprinted in 1693 and was possibly acted at Lincoln's Inn Fields in 1698–99; *The Comical Revenge* was reprinted in 1697 and may have been revived at this time. Music for two songs in *The Man of Mode* was published in January 1699, which suggests a new production 1698–99.

I would move on now to a consideration of the theme of *St Stephen's Green*, and its relation to the action. The major theme is suggested by the sub-title, *The Generous Lovers*. At the heart of the play lies a debate over the importance of money to a marriage. It is made plain that in the world that the play encompasses money defines social status. To have an estate is to be a gentleman. Even Vainly is tolerated because he is rich. On the other hand, Lady Volant has no status at all, since she is destitute. For Freelove to court Aemilia, therefore, as a penniless lover is regarded as the height of folly. It is not only the father-figure, Sir Francis, who takes this view but also Marina, Lady Volant, and Wormwood. Aemilia may call Marina "Mercenary" (I.i.49) for her attitude, but there is every reason to believe it to be the dominant social attitude: "I think a Good Estate is one of the prettiest Qualifications a Husband can have; my Love may decay, but an Estate is a certain Good" (I.i.51–3). Lady Volant puts it succinctly: "Oh Matrimony and Poverty join'd, are Comfortable Things! Sure his Head is as empty as his Pocket" (III.i. 178–80). It is left to Sir Francis, however, to underline the theme. He dismisses Freelove's notion of generosity, i.e., marriage for love alone. "Generous do you call it? Death! you make me mad. What a Pox is there no way to be thought Generous, but by becoming Mad and Begging" (III.i.388–90). He is insistent that Freelove is "mad" (line 392) in this matter. He also calls him "Romantick" (404), each term clearly implying one out of touch with reality. Philips places such stress on this reality that one must conclude that he was reflecting the society of his time. It was a time when insecurity drove people to pursuit of money in a way which was new, forging a new ethic. It was a transitional time, not yet dominated by the merchant class but bidding adieu to the aristocratic lifestyle which underlay the literary achievements of the Restoration period. The poise and grace of the Restoration lovers as they

appear in Etherege were yielding to anxiety, a pressure
that made the behaviour of the earlier generation seem
decadent. A debate about the significance of money would
not have appeared (and did not appear) in the comedies
of Etherege or Wycherley; but one finds it in Congreve,
writing in the sixteen nineties, for instance in *Love for
Love* (1695).

Now, as in the sixteen nineties, majority opinion would
probably agree with Sir Francis's point of view. It expresses
the modern, realistic view. Yet there is something in-
adequate, surely, about Marina's attitude, her assumption
that she can compensate for a loveless marriage by having
sufficient money to take a carriage for the Strand to look
out for "Conquests" (I.i.56). Bellmine's catalogue of house-
hold expenses, likewise, is so dreary as to raise the question
whether marriage is not more than accounting: "But you
know, Sir *Francis*, in Matrimonial Cases, we are to consider
how to maintain Children, and House-keeping, and a Wife
will expect a Coach, and a fine Equipage, and Gay Cloaths,
and—" which leads to Sir Francis's tired interjection, "And
the Devil and all, I know it Sir, I know it" (II.i.319–23).
Not that we are expected to find the starry-eyed protestations of Freelove preferable to the hardheaded business
sense of Sir Francis and "the world". For one thing, Freelove *is* 'moony' in such passages as, "I give my Heart
without Reserve, had I the World, I wou'd bestow it so"
(IV.i.346–7) and "To Love be all the Business of my Life;
it were abuse of Life to Live to any other End, be every
Moment so employ'd" (IV.i.358–60). This is what makes
him a comic figure, no doubt. But at the same time what
Sir Francis considers madness proves to be not only sane
but highly profitable. Freelove's generosity breeds a similar
generosity in Aemilia and virtue has a monetary reward.
This is the point the play firmly makes. It cheats, however,
inasmuch as Freelove and Aemilia had money all along.
They could afford the lofty ideals they promoted; they

were romantically 'slumming'. The element of fantasy in the play, especially in the resolution, weakens the serious implications of the major theme. *St Stephen's Green* is, after all, less realistic than *Love for Love*; it looks forward to the idealism and make-believe world of eighteenth-century comedy.

Placed in its wider context, *St Stephen's Green* is an interesting rather than an important comedy. By the year 1700 Restoration comedy had entered a new phase. Jeremy Collier had made his famous attack in *A Short View of the Immorality and Profaneness of the English Stage* in 1698, and whereas it is now usual to regard this attack as rather confirming existing changes in public taste than in initiating reforms, Collier helps to show how much *St Stephen's Green* was of its own day. In his Epistle Dedicatory Philips acknowledges the temper of the times: "In the Humour the present Age is, for a Man to own that he thinks Plays even lawful, 'tis almost enough to bring his Principles of Morality and Religion into Question." Here and in his Prologue Philips is at pains to emphasize the exemplary nature of his comedy. Times had changed, and a reaction had begun. The halcyon days of self-sufficient comedy, drama "beyond the diocese of the strict conscience", to use Lamb's famous description,[58] were over. It was strict conscience now, or nothing. A writer such as George Farquhar could still make his peace with the changing times, and produce comedies to compare with those of Etherege or Wycherley; but Philips was no Farquhar. Much less was he Congreve, whose last play, *The Way of the World*, was staged at roughly the same time as

58. Charles Lamb, "On the Artificial Comedy of the Last Century", in *Essays of Elia* (intro. by Augustine Birrell, London, n.d.), p. 289. Still useful as documentation on the mutation of Restoration into sentimental comedy is Joseph Wood Krutch, *Comedy and Conscience after the Restoration* (New York: Columbia University Press, 1924, 1949).

Philips's comedy. But weighed against a contemporary of lesser genius Philips is no disgrace. William Burnaby's comedy *The Reform'd Wife* was staged at Drury Lane during this season also (March 1700). It is a farcical, mildly satirical play, which flirts with the kind of material which earlier dramatists had manfully embraced. The ending, as the title implies, is entirely moral.[59] A detailed comparison with Philips's play would be tedious (the hero is called Freeman, Philips's hero is called Freelove, etc.). But it can be said that Philips's play is in no way inferior to Burnaby's. Each is a document of audience taste for the year 1700.

Turning now to the subject of Philips and Irish theatre, it may be repeated that the Dublin theatre modelled itself closely on London. The very idea of using St Stephen's Green as a focal point for a comedy is drawn from the many plays since the sixteen sixties which had Pall Mall or St James's Park as setting. It was an appropriate use of the local setting, however. St Stephen's Green had been developed between 1664 and 1670,[60] and thereafter it became a fashionable rendezvous. Early in the eighteenth century one finds this description: "St. *Stephen's Green* is a Mile about, is in a manner a Square, the Walks being wide and smooth; in good Weather the Quality of both Sexes make a gay Appearance, resembling the *English* Quality in the Mall in St. *James's Park*." [61] Malton's engraving presents

59. *The Reform'd Wife* is available in *The Dramatic Works of William Burnaby*, ed. F. E. Budd (London : Eric Partridge, 1931).

60. Edward MacLysaght, *Irish Life in the Seventeenth Century: After Cromwell*, second ed., revised and enlarged (Cork : University Press; Oxford : B. H. Blackwell, 1950), p. 234.

61. *A Description of the City of Dublin in Ireland . . . By a Citizen of* LONDON, *who liv'd twenty Years in Ireland* (London, 1732), pp. 25–6.

the later eighteenth-century view. It was not until 1880
that the modern park gardens were opened. In choosing
the green as central to his play, Philips found a symbol of
the society for whom he wrote. In later years, Yeats, Joyce,
Stephens and Flann O'Brien were to use the green for
setting or as image in an altogether different society.
Spanning the centuries, all the same, the green unites
Philips with the modern literary Dubliners.[62]
Philips sets all of the action either on the walks around
the green or indoors close by. No details are available as
to who painted the scenery, but the main view (of the
green) would have been a new piece. The other scenes,
Lady Volant's lodgings (act three) and Sir Francis's house
(V.ii.), could come out of stock. The view of the green
was still in use twenty years later, as Clark astutely notices.[63]
In Shadwell's *The Sham Prince* a fop called Sir Bullet Airy
calls on the two beaux Trueman and Welldon: "But come,
are you for *Stephen's Green*, 'tis a fine Morning, and there
will be a great deal of Company" (I.i) and in the next
scene the "Scene Changes to Stephen's-Green". (Incidentally, it is interesting to note the dropping of *Saint* from the
name of the green so early in its history.)
Besides the setting, there are some other instances of
local colour. There is reference to the Strand, a fashionable
promenade at this time. It extended for seven or eight miles
along the seashore on the north side of Dublin. John
Dunton took the air here during his visit to Dublin. In

62. See W. B. Yeats, *Explorations* (London : Macmillan, 1962)
pp. 222, 347; James Joyce, *A Portrait of the Artist as a
Young Man* (Harmondsworth : Penguin Books, 1970), pp. 184,
249. James Stephens, *The Charwoman's Daughter* (Dublin :
Gill and Macmillan, 1972), pp. 47, 53, 101; Flann O'Brien,
The Dalkey Archive (London : Pan Books, 1973), pp. 138, 187.
63. William Smith Clark, *The Early Irish Stage*, p. 148. The
scene of Charles Coffey's farce, *Wife and No Wife* (1724) is
also St Stephen's Green.

the play, Marina in anticipating the advantages of a
wealthy husband remarks: "Oh, 'tis such a Comfort!
When my Husband is in a Dogged Humour, to call for
my Glass Chariot, take the Air on the *Strand*, and make
half a score pleasant Visits, and as many Conquests"
(I.i.53–6). Bellmine also refers to it when speaking of his
assignation with Lady Volant: "She will no more fail
meeting me, than Mrs. *Flippant*, with her new Equipage,
wou'd miss the *Strand* on a *Sunday*" (IV.i.318–20). Again,
in the Epilogue (line 17) Lady Volant refers to Chapelizod,
or "Chappellizard" as Philips spells it, in association with
the Strand. It appears from this association that Chapelizod,
where the Lord Lieutenant had quarters, was also a
fashionable area, though the reference is certainly dubious.
Occasionally, there are topical allusions to Irish affairs,
such as "Rapparee Farthing" (V.i.86), an "Estate of Forfeited Lands" (V.ii.177), and "the Wool-Bill" (I.i.127).
Glosses on these and other such allusions will be found in
the notes to the text below. There is also the kind of local
reference that allows for or provokes a contrast with London. When Freelove takes the masked girls for women of
the town he draws from his friend the exclamation:
"Women of the Town! why, thou dost not know where
thou art. Women of the Town! why, there are no such
things in this Town" (I.i.326–8). A claim, of course, often
made since. Vainly and Lady Volant express negative views
of Dublin society: "this dull Town" (III.i.134), and
"Censorious Town" (III.i.430). This view extends later to
"this hideous Country" (V.ii.137–8). Bellmine, upon arrival
in Dublin, tries to impress the girls with the latest of
everything from London: "I have brought over some New
Fashions, New Tunes, and New Plays" (I.i.230–1). The
provincial attitude of some Dubliners begins to be satirized
in Bellmine's lines. The satire becomes more obvious when
Vainly is the one who boasts of England's advantages. He
welcomes the new arrivals as if come among savages:

"I am glad we have Gentlemen come to us now that understand Breeding and Conversation; 'Tis not to be had here. I protest, Sir, I am forced to go to *England* once a year, to refine my understanding" (III.i.234–8). Bellmine's retort is well taken. Since Vainly's understanding extends no further than his dress, "Cannot you keep a Correspondence with your Taylor?" and save himself the trip. It is left to Sir Francis, however, to squash Vainly for his downgrading of Ireland: "I can hold no longer. Why thou little worthless Contemptible Wretch! Do you entertain Strangers with your aversion for your Country, without being able to give one Reason for it[?]" (III.i.273–6).Dramatically, this stroke is effective. Less justified, but equally interesting, is the outburst from Trickwell when he meets his friend Timothy: "I have observ'd that none Despise *Ireland* so much as those who thrive best in it. And none are so severe in their Reflections upon it, as those who owe their Birth and Fortune to it; I have known many of 'em, when they come first to *London*, think there is no way so ready to purchase the Title of a Wit, as to Ridicule their own Country" (IV.i.17–23). A palpable hit from Philips here. This is the sort of comment that might lead to a genuine national awareness, if the cliché be permitted, and, in turn, a national literature.

It is important to realize how innovative Philips was in giving his play an Irish setting. Professional theatre in Ireland had been in existence only since 1637, barely forty years if one computes the years when the theatre was operating. Attempts at a specifically Irish drama were very few during that time. There was James Shirley's *St Patrick For Ireland*, staged at the Werburgh Street theatre in 1639. And there was *Landgartha*, by Dubliner Henry Burnell, staged the following year. Neither could be said to hold the mirror up to Irish life. The heroine of *Landgartha* is a Norwegian Amazon, offered to Dublin ladies, so the Epistle Dedicatorie says, as a model of chastity "and manly for-

titude in the female Sexe".[64] The only Irish reference
comes in a dance in *"an Irish Gowne tuck'd up to mid-
legge, with a broad basket-hilt Sword on"*. In another
country, such a dance would be called "Jim Crow". Philips,
at least, took his country seriously.

St Stephen's Green, then, is significant not only as an
indication of the new form comedy was taking at the end
of the seventeenth century, "a laundered form of the old
comedy",[65] perhaps, but also because of its depiction of
Ireland for an Irish audience. Philips found a true successor
in Charles Shadwell, who first came to Dublin in 1713 and
thereafter wrote several plays with Irish settings.[66] Some of
these were comedies in the manner of Philips's play, and
one was an historical tragedy, *Rotherick O'Connor*, which
may in turn have given the cue to Philips for his *Hibernia
Freed*. With these two writers, whatever their faults, is to
be found the real beginning of Ireland's dramatic tradition.
As the eighteenth century progressed they found successors
in Thomas Sheridan and Charles Macklin, who tried at
least once to offer an Irish point of view.[67] But, in general,
the spirit which might have established a native drama was
lacking. The experience of an anonymous playwright in
the year 1804 sums up the reason why. He had written

64. *Landgartha. A Tragie-Comedy, as it was presented in the
new Theater in Dublin, with good applause, being an Ancient
story*, written by H. B. (Dublin, 1641).
65. Robert D. Hume's description of the changing comedy of
the 1690s fits *St Stephen's Green* very well, although Hume
does not mention the play. See *The Development of English
Drama in the Late Seventeenth Century*, p. 435.
66. See William Smith Clark, *The Early Irish Stage*, pp.
158–74. The plays were published in *The Works of Mr.
Charles Shadwell* (2 vols., Dublin, 1720).
67. Thomas Sheridan's *The Brave Irishman* was staged at
Smock Alley in 1743; Charles Macklin's *The True-Born
Irishman* was staged at the Crow Street Theatre in 1762.

his comedy, *All at Home; or, the Irish Nieces,* for the Dublin stage because so few "have chosen to lay the scene of action in this country" and he thought it should be feasible to present characters "wholly Irish" and yet "to avoid political, national, or personal ideas".[68] The Dublin theatre managers rejected his play, the author continues, "because, as was alleged, it had not gone through the ordeal of a London audience". Boucicault was to change some of this, but it was left to Yeats, Lady Gregory and Edward Martyn to tackle the fundamental problem by making the theatre truly Irish, the expression of the native population and its culture. In so doing, they were really extending Philips's concern far beyond anything he had ever conceived.

68. Preface to *All at Home; or, The Irish Nieces. A Comedy, in Five Acts* (Dublin, 1904), A3—A3v.

NOTE ON THE TEXT

St Stephen's Green, or, the Generous Lovers was printed in Dublin by John Brocas in 1700. The wording on the title page suggests that publication coincided with stage production: "As it is Acted at / The Theatre-Royal, / IN / DUBLIN." No other edition has been traced. The *New Cambridge Bibliography of English Literature* mentions a London edition of 1720, but this appears to be an error.[1] The error may be derived from Allardyce Nicoll, since he earlier gave information of such an edition in his *A History of English Drama 1600–1900*. In his list of plays, Nicoll also says that *St Stephen's Green* was published anonymously in Dublin in 1700.[2] He cannot have seen a copy of the text, since the author's name appears both on the title page and Epistle Dedicatory. If there were an edition in London in 1720 this would certainly suggest a London production at this time. No evidence for a London production exists.

Eight copies of John Brocas's printed text have been found. These are in the Bodleian Library, the British Library, Dublin City Libraries (two copies), the Henry E. Huntington Library, the National Library of Ireland, and the library of Trinity College, Dublin (two copies). The present text is that of the copy in the National Library of Ireland. All of the other copies have been consulted. No variants have been found.

The text is a quarto edition, A4—L4, the play itself paginated from B onwards, pp. 1–80. The text of one of

1. *The New Cambridge Bibliography of English Literature*, II (1660–1800), ed. George Watson (Cambridge : University Press, 1971), 797. The entry also states that the Dublin edition of *St Stephen's Green* was anonymous.

2. Allardyce Nicoll, *A History of English Drama 1660–1900*, II, *Early Eighteenth Century Drama* (Cambridge : University Press, 1969), 349.

the copies in the Dublin City Libraries (Pearse Street) lacks the matter prior to B. A peculiarity in the running title (actually the sub-title) in all copies is that the article is sometimes italic and sometimes roman, in an irregular way. It is roman on pp. 3, 5, 7, 13, 15, 17, 23, 25, 31, 33, 39, 41, 45, 49, 53, 57, 61, 65, 69, 75 and 79; italic on pp. 9, 11, 19, 21, 27, 29, 35, 37, 43, 47, 51, 55, 59, 63, 67, 71, 73 and 77. This irregularity is not reflected elsewhere in the text.

Brocas's edition is a good one, with very few errors. These have been silently corrected, since they are both minor and infrequent. For example, in the Prologue, line 8 reads *"And equal Share of Wit to him has giv'n"* where *"An"* is obviously meant. Punctuation marks were very occasionally either omitted or obviously in error, and to amend without noting the error seems the best course in such cases. The letter 's' has been substituted for the old 'ſ' throughout, and 'W' for 'VV'. The Epilogue, which in the 1700 quarto is printed A4 *recto* following the Prologue (A3 *verso*), is here placed after the text of the play. For the convenience of the reader the names of the characters are given in full throughout. Occasionally, the stage directions in the quarto are in error or are inconsistent; these have been corrected so that all stage directions except those for entrances now appear at the right-hand margin and square brackets have been omitted. (Where used in the present edition square brackets indicate interpolated material.) In the quarto, directions for the 'aside' are usually placed after the speech, and in accordance with customary editorial practice these indications are here placed before the speech. The rhyming lines which appear at the end of each act have been printed in italics, consistent with the printing of verse in the Prologue and Epilogue; the same may be said of the two lines from a song used in IV.i.196–7. In all other respects, in spelling, punctuation and capitalization for example, the original text has been followed.

Line numbers have been added in the margin of each page, however, and these are referred to in the commentary on the text in the Introduction and in the Notes. Although rhyming couplets appear within acts two and four (at II.i.350–1 and at IV.i.282–3) no change of scene is called for, and I have therefore regarded the action as continuous. It is only in act five that I have considered it proper to provide for a new scene within the act, at line 203.

To be mentioned also is a manuscript transcription of *St Stephen's Green* which is in the Gilbert Collection, Dublin City Libraries. The title page reads: Sᵗ STEPHENS GREEN; / OR   THE / GENEROUS   LOVERS. / A / COMEDY / IN / FIVE ACTS. / The author's name is omitted. The manuscript is in octavo, with eighty-seven numbered pages, and it contains title page, Dramatis Personae, and the play. It omits Prologue, Epilogue, Epistle Dedicatory and part of one scene, to be described below. Otherwise, this is a faithful copy of Brocas's text, apart from modifications of spelling, capitalization and punctuation. According to the Gilbert catalogue, the MS is "Apparently in a late eighteenth century hand".[3] The MS is bound in leather, with marbled boards, and has on the spine, "Sᵗ STEPHENS GREEN."

On page eighty, the MS jumps over a crucial scene. After Trickwell's exit (V.i.200) the next line given is Sir Francis Feignyouth's, "Oh are you there!" (V.ii.108). Over one hundred lines are omitted, dealing with Sir Francis's marriage celebrations (including the song). As it is obviously a deliberate omission one can only conclude that the transcriber disapproved of the material at this point, the one moderately bawdy passage in the whole play. Perhaps he

3. *Catalogue of the Books & Manuscripts Comprising the Library of the late Sir John T. Gilbert* . . . Compiled by Douglas Hyde, LL.D. & D. J. O'Donoghue (Dublin : Browne and Nolan, 1918), p. 951.

intended the play for family reading. It is ironic, certainly, to find Philips's play, which is painstakingly proper if placed beside the most famous of the Restoration comedies, being censored a hundred years after he wrote it. Yet, at least the MS shows that Philips's play was not entirely forgotten in later years, even if the author himself was pushed off the title page, almost into oblivion.

St. Stephen's-Green

OR THE

Generous LOVERS.

A

COMEDY,

As it is Acted at

The Theatre - Royal,

IN

DUBLIN.

Written by *WILL. PHILIPS*, Esq;

DUBLIN,

Printed by *John Brocas* in *School-House-Lane* ;
And are to be Sold by the Booksellers, 1700.

To the Right Honourable

The Earl of Inchiquin

My Lord,

THIS Play has a double Reason for seeking Shelter under Your Lordship; I Writ it, and for our *Irish* Stage, and You are the chief Friend which either has: But I shou'd be Cautious in Declaring what 'tis probable the World may Condemn in you; since in the Humour the present Age is, for a Man to own that he thinks Plays even lawful, 'tis almost enough to bring his Principles of Morality and Religion into Question. But, My Lord, the Firmness of yours is so well known, that I shall have no Reason to forbear saying, you have an Esteem for Plays; and I may, with Safety to your Reputation, Applaud you for it, since I am Confident the greatest Zealot wou'd slacken his Fury against the Stage, and join with you in Supporting it, did he know how earnestly you Wish it Reform'd from the Corruption of Manners, to the Encouraging Virtue, and Ex-

10

posing Vice; and with what Decency, Modesty, and
Good Breeding, you wou'd have it Regulated. You may
remember you Caution'd me to observe these Things,
20   when I first acquainted you that I had a Design to
Write this Comedy, and I have attempted to Obey
you. I wish Your Lordship had given me farther
Instructions; then, this wou'd have appear'd more
Perfect and Correct to the World, and an Offering
more Worthy you. As it is, I present it to you with
Courage, because I know, the Errors your Judgment
discerns, your Goodness will Excuse, and what you
cannot Excuse you will at least Forgive. I only Wish
there may be something in it, which may prevent your
30   Blushing while you Protect it, and shall very readily
own the Faults the Criticks find in it; I have not yet
heard them, but without doubt there are many, and
therefore I think my self the more obliged to those who
have been so particurly kind to this Play. They have
sufficiently evidenced how Inclinable they are to Encourage Wit and Poetry, by being so Favourable and
so Generous to my weak Attempts on both; who have
so little of the one, and so unskill'd in the other. I shou'd
be extreamly pleas'd, if my Success wou'd move any
40   other who has a happier Genius, to divert this Town
with some Performance of this kind. But it is my
Satisfaction and Pride, that tho' he shou'd Write better,
he cannot meet with more Encouragement than I have
done. And since I own my Weakness, and yet boast of
Success, you may be assur'd, that as I think my self
Answerable for the former, so I know the latter is
owing to your Lordship; another Proof of your accustomed Goodness, and a fresh Obligation to me. But
this is a Subject I must not pursue, for tho' the acknow-

ledgement of Obligations is but a small Return, yet I 50
know you think it too much; and therefore tho' Silence
is a Pain to the Grateful, yet I choose to be uneasy to
my self, rather than offensive to your Modesty, which I
know will not Pardon my Publishing, what you will not
allow me even to mention when we are together. Give
me leave only, My Lord, to assure you that I have a
just Sense of your Favours, and that tho' I had ne're
receiv'd one, yet I shou'd ever have been

My Lord,

Your Lordship's

Most Faithful and most Humble Servant,

Will. Philips.

Dramatis Personae

Freelove, A Gentleman of *England* ⎫
Bellmine, A Gentleman of *Ireland* ⎭ Friends.

Sir *Francis Feignyouth*, Old and Amorous.

Wormwood, Snarling and Ill-natur'd.

Vainly, A Pert Conceited Fop.

Trickwell, Servant to *Freelove*.

Timothy Tellpenny, Steward to Lady *Volant*.

Æmilia, Niece to Sir *Francis Feignyouth*.

Marina, His Daughter.

Lady *Volant*, Affected and Mercinary.

PROLOGUE.

HOW hard's the Fate which Poetry attends,
When ev'ry Man to be its Judge Pretends.
Not so in other Arts; Painters best tell
Which Colour, Shade, or Posture does excel.
Doctors a Right to Kill or Save obtain;
And Lawyers only do the Law Explain.
But ev'ry Fool fancies indulgent Heav'n
An equal Share of Wit to him has giv'n.
And talks of Time, Place, Action, and the Plot,
Words, like a Parrot, he by rote has got.   10
Hither such come to Censure, not to Hear,
And whisper dull Remarks in's Neighbour's Ear.
Chat the whole Play, then Judgment give at Guess,
And damn the Poet for the Actor's dress.
Strut in the Pit, Survey the Gallery,
In hopes to be lur'd up by some kind She.
Humours still opposite to ours they have,
Laugh when we weep; and when we laugh look grave.
Our Author hopes none such are here to Day,
For they'll ne're relish this Dull, Sober Play.   20
Where there's not one Immodest Word to move
In the Box Blushes, or a Laugh above.
But for their Comfort, tho' the Scene be here,
The Characters of Vice he takes elsewhere.
If any to themselves Reflections take,
They are to Blame who Applications make.

St. Stephen's-Green

OR,

The Generous Lovers.

ACT I

SCENE St. *Stephen's-Green.*

Enter Æmilia *and* Marina

Marina. WELL, well, *Æmilia,* You may pretend what you please; But I am sure, You go to Church thus constantly, only to Pray for an Easterly Wind.

Æmilia. Truly *Marina,* if my Love has made me Devout, yours has made you very Lazy; for ever since you saw *Bellmine,* you are grown as fond of your Bed, as a young Poet is of his first Works.

Marina. And is not that a properer place to think of one's Lover, than the Church? I am as much teaz'd with your Devotion, as a Rake is with Dunns, or as a Mask in the Play-House is, with that Rake. 10

Æmilia. Love that sweetens all Tempers, has sowr'd thine.

Marina. Pray let me hear no more of it then.

Æmilia. And yet if I should Talk of any thing else, you would no more mind me, than our Gallery does the Parson. What! Last Pacquet brought you no Letters? Why, he's Coming.

Marina. So is *Freelove*; That makes you so Gay. But Dear *Æmilia,* now I have mention'd him, inform me better of his

20 Character, and tell me how you came acquainted with him, for he must be an Extraordinary Person that cou'd please you.

Æmilia. While I waited for a Wind at *Chester*, he chanc'd to come thither. He saw me, and it seems I displeas'd him not. He quickly found an opportunity to be acquainted, since I did not shun it; for I own at first view I lik'd him.

Marina. How, at first View! What! You that such Numbers have sigh'd for, and have been insensible to all; Like at sight!

Æmilia. 'Twere a Wrong to Friendship, and Beneath me,
30 to dissemble with you. His Person pleas'd me; but when he talk'd, his Discourse appear'd so Soft, so Natural; his Wit so Lively and so Unconstrain'd; That, tho' I ever Dreaded the Inconveniences of Love, I struggled harder to conceal my Flame, than to restrain my Heart; for having Seen and Heard, 'twas mine no more.

Marina. Meer Rapture! But what Reputation has he in the World? For I regard that more than his Person or Wit.

Æmilia. As I, so he, was to most a Stranger. All agreed he had no Estate, but a Fine Gentleman.

40 *Marina.* How's that! No Estate, and a Fine Gentleman! Advise him to keep where he is, if he would preserve that Character. I assure you, 'tis as Difficult to be thought so here, without an Estate; as it is to be thought Honest and Get one.

Æmilia. All are not of that Opinion; for if *Bellmine* had no Fortune, I suppose you wou'd think him a Fine Gentleman.

Marina. I thank Heaven he has a very good one, and really Cousin, I find it much for his Interest in my Heart, that I never Considered him without One.

Æmilia. You are Mercenary.

50 *Marina.* Not wholly so; perhaps I shou'd not esteem an acquaintance the worse; But I think a Good Estate is one of the prettiest Qualifications a Husband can have; my Love may decay, but an Estate is a certain Good. Oh, 'tis such a Comfort! When my Husband is in a Dogged Humour, to call for my Glass Chariot, take the Air on the *Strand*, and make

half a score pleasant Visits, and as many Conquests.

Æmilia. Conquests! I hope you wou'd not receive Addresses if you were Married?

Marina. Not Bare-fac'd Love, not Plain so; but certainly nothing pleases us more, than to be Admir'd; pleases us! 60 pleases every Thing; What thing is not pleas'd to be Lik'd? Then 'tis a certain Cure for the Spleen. Can any thing be more Diverting than to have a Man who has ten times more Wit than I have, fall at my Feet, and Adore mine?

Æmilia. Can you think so, and not conclude it Flattery?

Marina. Flattery! What then? Is not my Power still the Greater, to force him to say, what he does not think? Then I make my Husband Jealous by it.

Æmilia. Is that an Advantage?

Marina. Oh a Great One! I have known it sharpen many 70 a Stomach that was Cloy'd before. At Least, if Jealousie will not make him Kind, 'twill make him Civil, out of fear of what I may do; Nay, I think it shou'd make him Proud too.

Æmilia. There is indeed a secret pleasure in having our Choice approv'd of; and I never knew a Man fond of his Wife, when she was slighted by others. He will no more boast of his Choice then, than she with Reason will boast of her Virtue. And it seems then, you do not doubt being Admir'd.

Marina. Truly *Æmilia*, I fancy this Face, Bad as it is, with the advantage of Gay Cloaths, Coach and Equipage, will 80 draw Admirers, where there are so many Stait Fellows in Red out of Employment.

Æmilia. Fy, fy, You begin to talk madly; come, let's haste to Church, and drive away these Thoughts; I believe they have almost done.

Marina. Well, Thou art the strangest Creature; You are always interrupting my Mirth with Church, and at Church I am sure you are thinking of something else.—Come prithee, Let us take t'other Turn—What you will go—Well I follow.

Exeunt.

Enter Freelove, Bellmine *and* Trickwell, *as newly Arriv'd.*

90   *Freelove.* We have had a pleasant Quick Passage. Wou'd
there were no more Shelves, nor Quicksands, no more Diffi-
culties in my Voyage of Love, and that it might be as soon
finish'd.

Bellmine. I am sure I have been aboard long enough to
smell like one of the Cabbin Boys; I fancy I totter still; the
Ground seems to rise in Waves before me, and when I walk,
I lift my Feet and Paw like a Horse who has just lost his sight.

Freelove. (*Looking about*) A pleasant place this! The Name
of it?

100   *Bellmine.* St. *Stephen's-Green.*

Freelove. I like the Air.—I am glad your House has the
benefit of it. Here Sirrah————what, you are Surveying
where you shall get Drunk to Night; this Rogue looks out for
a Brandy Shop with more Earnestness and Joy, than a
Privateer for a Merchant Man. I wonder *Bellmine* you dare
trust this Drunken Rogue with so many weighty Affairs.

Trickwell. Alas Sir, Your Worship knows, I am the soberest
Man alive: But if ever I do drink, 'tis always after I have
dispatch'd my Business, I divide my time well.

110   *Freelove.* Oh yes! Exceeding well! Between Drinking for
your Diversion, and Pimping for his. But while you are Sober,
and before he has any New Honourable Employment for you,
go see that our Things are brought from Ship-board. We shall
walk here till you return.   *Exit* Trickwell.

Bellmine. If all my Old Friends have not forgot me, I hope
to employ him.

Freelove. I thought this last Amour wou'd have made a
Convert of thee, and Cur'd thee of all Extravagancies.

Bellmine. This last Amour has Quite spoyl'd thee; thou
120   wer't once one of the prettiest Fellows about the Town; thy
Advice assisted me in Love, thy Wit promoted Drinking, thy
Example Encourag'd both; But now thou art Grown a Downright Damn'd, Sober, Dull, Virtuous Fellow.

Freelove. Well, You are upon the Brink of Matrimony; if it
does not Cure thee, 'twill at least tame thee.

Bellmine. Oh for Heaven's sake Name it not! I dread it as much as our Farmers do the Wool-Bill.

Freelove. If you have such terrible apprehensions of it; How came you to think on't?

Bellmine. Think on't! Why I don't think on't; nor ever will 130 think on't. If I Repent, which 'tis a thousand to one but I shall, I am Resolv'd to have that Excuse, that I Marry'd inconsiderately.

Freelove. 'Tis as extravagant and unaccountable for a Man of your Sentiments, and loose Life, to Marry, as for a Coward with a good Estate to turn Souldier; Yet I have seen both; and as in an Engagement, they Wink and Dye, so you'll Wink and Marry.

Bellmine. I beseech you, no more of it. I hate the word, Marriage, as much as a Mariner does whistling at Sea; and 140 for the same Reason, I fancy it will raise Stormy Weather. 'Tis a hard Case that we must submit to the thing we Hate, before we can have the Woman we Love.

Freelove. The Ladies have a much harder Case with Men of your Extravagant Principles: You are always Teazing 'em with Love; if they Return it, you Insult; if they Refuse it, you Rail; if they Marry you, you grow weary of them; if they Comply without it, you Contemn them.

Bellmine. *Æmilia* has made you a Rare Advocate for the Sex; I have known the time, when you wou'd no more allow 150 Virtue in Womankind, than Honesty in a Jesuit, or Sincerity in a Courtier.

Freelove. Whenever you hear any Man talk so, take it for Granted, that he has lately met with some Disappointment; or that he is more Conversant with the Bottle than with them; and 'tis then we chiefly deny them to be Virtuous, when we find they are so: For some of you prudent Sparks, never Commend a Woman, but to Conceal an Intrigue with her; and the readiest way to ruin their Reputation, is for such to give her a good Character. 160

Bellmine. I confess I have more Charity for them since I

knew *Marina*, than formerly; and you are giving a sufficient Proof of your good Opinion of the Sex, and of the Violence of your Love, that have come from *London* hither, to Marry a Lady without a Fortune.

Freelove. And wou'd think my Travel round the Earth Rewarded with a Look.

Bellmine. I know I please you, by daily asking her Character.

170 *Freelove.* My Heart is never Easy, while my Tongue is employ'd about any other Subject. She has Goodness without Folly or Easiness; Wit and Virtue without ill Nature or Vanity; Beauty without Art or Affectation: She is so Excellent, that even her own Sex Admires her, for those very Charms which Create their Envy.

Bellmine. Young, I don't doubt.

Freelove. She is so Young, she wou'd not take it Ill, to be call'd Old.

Bellmine. But has she such an entire Possession of your 180 Heart, that you can make Love to no other?

Freelove. I cou'd not even Affect it.

Bellmine. I can, as you shall see immediately; for I perceive some Ladies coming this way Mask'd.

Freelove. Well, I'll give you an Opportunity and Leave you.

Bellmine. No, to give me an Opportunity, you must stay; Engage one, while I talk to the other.

Freelove. You must Excuse me.

Bellmine. Away; Thou art Grown as Surly, as if thou wer't already Married; Come, no Denial, walk on a little, we'll 190 take a short Turn and Meet them.   *Exeunt.*

Enter Æmilia and Marina.

Marina. Now as I live Cousin our Prayers are heard; Yonder is certainly my Spark *Bellmine.*

Æmilia. And with him *Freelove* ! How my Heart beats and labours in my Breast ! And now my Blood has taken the Alarm, flies to its Spring to be Assistant there, forsakes its

Channels, and leaves each distant part Pale and Faint.

Marina. Pale and Faint! That is pleasant! Now am I ten
times more Lively than I was; my Heart is a little Unruly
too; But that is only, because it is weary of this Old Dull
Prison, and has a mind to exchange Quarters with that   200
Gentleman's. Prithee don't stand Trembling here, but let us
walk towards 'em.

Æmilia. Marina, Hold! I must be recovered a little before
I own my self: But what say you, if we shou'd keep on our
Masks, and see if they will Attack us; we shall try their
Constancy by it.

Marina. Nay, as for Constancy, I am not so Unreasonable
as to expect that yet. 'Twill be very well, if my Spark leaves
Rambling to a half Crown Ordinary abroad, when he has a
plentiful Feast provided for him at home. However, I like the   210
Proposal, I shall try his Wit, and Rally him by it: And
Nothing pleases me more than making an Ass of a Man of
Wit; and a Mask is a Rare Opportunity, it Conceals who we
are, and Encourages us to be Bold, while our Sex Protects us.

Re-enter Freelove *and* Bellmine.

Bellmine. Ladies your Servant! We think our selves very
Fortunate, That the first we see have so fine a Mien and
Shape, and I am confident your Faces are answerable: Will
not you have the good Nature as to Unmask, and prove me in
the Right?

Marina. A good reasonable Request truly in your first   220
Speech: Are the Ladies of your Acquaintance so very Coming? But you are as much Strangers to us in Expecting it, as
you are to the place by Demanding it.

Bellmine. You like us the worse it may be for being so?

Marina. That supposition shews you are Strangers, or you
wou'd know, that to be so, is a recommendation here.

Bellmine. Does that humour reign here? I hope it does in
you too; then I may succeed; for I assure you I am but this
moment arriv'd; and to make me still the more acceptable to

230 thee, my Pretty Dear Creature; know, that I have brought
over some New Fashions, New Tunes, and New Plays; I can
tell you which House has the best Audience, which Player is
most Applauded; who the Celebrated Beauty of the Town,
who keeps the best Equipage; I can tell you who Loves who,
and who does worse; what Duels have been lately Fought;
who Kill'd, who Hang'd, who Jilted, who Married, who——
    Marina. And so Convince me, you go abroad for the same
wise Intent, most of our young Sparks do. But you may as
soon Borrow Money of a grave Citizen, by this Character of
240 your self, as expect any Favour from me by it.
    Bellmine. Will not this please you? why then I can give
you an account of the Court; I can tell you which Lord has
the greatest Levy; I can tell you of great Favourites, who
scarce cou'd Breathe for Crowds of servile Sycophants, and in
a days time as lonely as if it had been Writ over their Doors,
"This House is Infected with the Plague." I can tell you of
the Advancement of Fools and Knaves, and the Disgrace of
Men of Sense [and] Worth, I can——
    Marina. Hold, hold, you will only perswade me you have
250 met with some Disappointment there, for few rail at the
Court for any other Reason.
    Bellmine. Let me but have one stroke at Rogues in Power——
    Marina. Not a Syllable, or I shall believe you are vext,
because you cannot be one in your turn.
    Bellmine. Will not this do? why then have at the Parlia-
ment——
    Marina. Worse and worse.
    Bellmine. Nay then, I find no subject will please you but
Love; and the tender soft Things I have to say on that, must
260 be whisper'd.
    Freelove. A pretty New Way your Ladyship has of Rallying
truly. You think Flattery too great a Good to be enjoy'd by
Men only, and I'll lay my Life if once you aim at it, you
will be too hard for us, 'tis said we cannot keep pace with you
in Virtue, I am sure you outstrip us in Vice, when once you

set your selves to it.

Æmilia. 'Twere very unhappy a Man of your Wit and Judgment should have a mean Opinion of us.

Freelove. My Wit and Judgment! very pretty. Take my Advice, never Admire a Man for those Qualifications, which 270 I assure you are the greatest Enemies imaginable to your Sex. Wit and Judgment! why a Man must prove he has neither, before you'll allow him to be in Love.

Æmilia. You harbour severe Thoughts of us, and Love.

Freelove. I seldom speak my Thoughts to a Mask; But for once, to Convince you I have Charitable Thoughts of both; I'll venture to tell you I am in Love.

Æmilia. I fancy then your Mistress treats you with severity, or requires unreasonable things of you.

Freelove. There is nothing she requires I can think so. 280

Æmilia. If she be unkind, try another; I am confident so fine a Gentleman must succeed.

Freelove. You are so very lavish in your Praises, that I know you expect I shou'd proffer you a Bottle of Wine and a cold Chicken.

Æmelia. My Praises at least deserve a civiller Reply.

Freelove. Nay if you knew with what indifference I proffer it; you wou'd have more reason to affect an angry Tone; for if you shou'd comply, I assure you my usage shou'd be much Civiller than possibly you expect. 290

Æmelia. Come, this ill Nature is meer affectation in you; you have so good an Appearance, I am resolv'd to esteem you, spite of your indifference.

Freelove. I am sorry, Madam, my indifference has not the same effect on you, that your forwardness has on me. Here *Bellmine*, prithee relieve me; I am the dullest Fellow at this Common-place Chat.

Marina. You have done very Charitably, Sir, to call to your Friend; Poor Gentleman! he has ran himself clear out of 300 Breath by Protesting his Passion for me.

Bellmine. Who I, Madam? alas, I have said nothing yet;

why Madam, if I do not admire your Wit, your Shape, your Mien, the colour of your Hair, your Fancy in your Dress, more than——

Marina. Have a Care what you say, Sir; pray let your Simile be short, for I fancy you are so very Fickle, that before you have made an end of it, your mind may change.

Æmilia. Well, we will give the Gentleman leisure to reflect till Evening, and perhaps by that time his Friend may be in
310 a better Humour.

Bellmine. Dear, Kind, Obliging Creature, we will certainly attend ye.   *Exeunt Women.*
Why, what a damn'd unlucky Rogue was I now? that I did not attack her: she seems to be half won already, and I'll engage you did not say one kind passionate thing to her.

Freelove. Not a Syllable truly.

Bellmine. And she was very Compliant?

Freelove. So she seem'd.

Bellmine. Why there's it now. Oh Fortune, Fortune! how
320 dost thou shower Wealth upon the Rich?

Freelove. You have great reason to complain of Fortune indeed, because you have not succeeded with such as these!

Bellmine. Such as these! why, who do you take 'em for, pray?

Freelove. For Women of the Town.

Bellmine. Women of the Town! why, thou dost not know where thou art. Women of the Town! why, there are no such things in this Town.

Freelove. No! then I have found the Reason you spend so
330 little time in your own Country.

Bellmine. *Freelove*, not a word more of my Extravagancies as you tender my Pleasures; I am not so much Reform'd yet, but I have a Mind to enjoy them a little farther, and I cannot do that here, but under the Disguise of a Sober, Discreet Person.

Freelove. And so you wou'd be thought Virtuous, that you may be the more Conveniently Wicked.

Bellmine. Even so Faith.

Freelove. A very pious Design truly! yet I have known you affect a quite contrary Reputation, and were industrious to 340 be thought a very Lewd Fellow; Nay, and I have known such a Character do a Man effectual Service with Women.

Bellmine. Ay, where Opportunities were easily met with; Womens Inclinations are alike in all places, but all Places are not alike. In *London,* 'tis difficult to be known; here, impossible to be conceal'd. Such a Character may do one Service with the Woman, but not with her Relations. There, you may make a thousand Cuckolds, yet they never hear of your Name: Here, you cannot make one without being Intimate with him; and I'll undertake you shall not be three days in 350 Town, but every Body in Town will know you; nay, and know, whence you came, how long you stay, what's your Business, and if you have none, they will feign enough for you; for I could name you such a Sett, so Inquisitive, such Detractors——But hold, yonder comes one will spare my pains.

Freelove. Who, that Old Fellow?

Bellmine. He's their President: One who never spoke Commendably of any Mortal. There are no Degrees of Good with him, only some are less Bad than others; and indeed he has 360 reason to talk, for he has been a Bubble to Man and Woman from his Infancy.

Freelove. Methinks his ill Nature shou'd prevent him from that.

Bellmine. His ill Nature prevents him from designing to oblige any one, but he has so good an Opinion of his own Wisdom, that any one may make as Ass of him. Scurrility with him, is giving an Impartial Character, and that you may think he speaks Truth, he rails most at those of his own 370 temper.

Freelove. Enough of him; Pray let me avoid being known to him.

Bellmine. Impossible; I'll undertake, tho' we have not been

Landed these two hours, he has had an account of it already;
and comes to Congratulate our Arrival, for he will be tolerably civil to the present Company, either out of fear, or
design to gather something he may rail at.

Enter Wormwood.

Wormwood. Mr. *Bellmine,* Your humble Servant.
Bellmine. Your Servant, Mr. *Wormwood.*
380 *Wormwood.* I am glad to see you in your own Country
again; I heard you were come.
Bellmine. Freelove, d'ye hear?
Wormwood. I was told too there is an English Gentleman,
your Friend, accompany'd you hither : I suppose that may
be he. Prithee what may be his Business? they say he is
come to——
Bellmine. What, know his Business already! Come, I'll
present you to him, and you may know it from himself. Mr.
Freelove be pleas'd to know this Gentleman; he is a plain
390 Impartial Historian of the Times, and a very proper Acquaintance for a Stranger; for he knows the whole Town, and
gives every one their just Character.
Wormwood. Why truly, Sir, as this Gentleman says, I do
speak my Mind; I think no Body can tax me with Flattery.
Freelove. You shou'd bid him have a care of Detraction too.
Bellmine. (Apart) You'll spoil all, if he hears you you'll
terrify him into good Nature. [*Aloud*] No, he hates Detraction
too; for 'tis not Detraction to speak ill of those who deserve it.
Wormwood. You are in the right, Sir, and that I wou'd do,
400 tho' it were of a Judge, and I had a Suit depending : I wou'd
sooner loose my Cause, than my honest way of Speaking.
Freelove. I believe you will be more Entertaining to this
Gentleman, if you will tell him who are the Beauties of the
Town.
Wormwood. If you will rely on the Ladies Characters of
one another, there are none. For they are so Envious here
(for which you must know I hate 'em) that each thinks the

Commendation of another is a wrong done to her self, and that you deprive her of that Beauty you approve of in another.

Freelove. I have heard there were many fine Women in this 410 Town.

Wormwood. It may be so; But you who are a young Gentleman, and I suppose would be acceptable to them, must have a care of saying so.

Freelove. Why so?

Wormwood. Because you must make your Court to the present, by railing at the absent.

Freelove. That is a New Way indeed.

Wormwood. An infallible Way to succeed. 'Tis what they practice to one another. I can name you some Women who 420 visit and are visited by half the Town, are civilly treated, and have no Merit but Impudence and Scurrility. As for Example——

Bellmine. Have a care of Names.

Wormwood. I'll venture at hers. My Lady *Volant.*——

Bellmine. How, my Lady *Volant*! I never saw her, but have heard abundance of her. And is she in Being still! why what a bottomless sink of Malice is her Breast, that is not yet exhausted?

Wormwood. 'Tis a Corrupted one, and taints every thing 430 comes within it. She hates every Body, yet is the civilest Person in the whole World, when she wou'd dive into your Affairs.

Bellmine. Or wou'd borrow a Guinea. However she is a good Manager; for her Lodging and Dyet cost her Nothing; she Bilks one, and Spunges for t'other.

Wormwood. I see you can Rail too.

Bellmine. Oh she's a publick Pest. She has done more harm to deserving young Ladies Reputations, than the Small Pox has to their Faces.

Freelove. No more of her, I beseech you. But is there no 440 Body Merits a Good Character?

Wormwood. You that are a Stranger may think there is. But those who deserve to be Laugh'd at next, are that Young,

Pert, Conceited Fool *Vainly*, who construes every Abuse a Complement, and that old Lewd, Fat, Doting *Feignyouth*, who are both bewitch'd by her Ladyship.

Bellmine. How, Sir *Francis Feignyouth*?

Wormwood. The same. He fancies her Virtuous and Rich, tho' she has so very little of either, she wou'd renounce her
450 Virtue to borrow a Crown. And because she is reserv'd to him, he concludes she is so to every Body else.

Bellmine. This is Incredible. Is it possible he can be ignorant of her Character? he has Friends enough to inform him.

Wormwood. If you went about to inform him, you wou'd find it a hard Matter to convince him of your Friendship; For he believes whoever speaks against her, has some design on her himself. As for *Vainly*, I think no Body values him enough to advise him.

Bellmine. What if I shou'd advise Sir *Francis*; he cannot
460 believe I have a design on her.

Wormwood. But he knows you have one on his Daughter *Marina*, and he'll imagine you advise out of Interest.

Bellmine. Well, Sir, I thank you for your Information, it may be of use to me. Will you please to Dine with us at the *Globe*; and let us know more of the Affairs of the Town. Come *Freelove*, I see your Man yonder, I suppose he has taken care of our Things; we'll Dine and change our Cloaths, and then take another Turn here.

Freelove. I suppose your Design is to meet your Masks again;
470   *But have a care, this unknown Face may prove*
        Of Force, to overcome your former Love.
        You wear a brittle and an easy Chain,
        Who can to other Objects Passion Feign.
Bel. *No, I can Feign, and yet my Heart defend.*
Free. *You're lost if on your own Strength you depend.*
        The Stratagems and Force of Womens Eyes
        Subdue the Strong, Ensnare, and Fool the Wise.
                                        Exeunt.

ACT II

Scene Continues.

Enter Wormwood.

Wormwood. **P**OX on this troublesome Coxcomb, he follows me again, there is no getting from him. If I abuse him, he thinks 'tis either Raillery, or like a Friend to tell him of his Faults.

Enter Vainly.

Vainly. I ask your Pardon, Sir, for staying behind you, but I cou'd not help it. You saw the Occasion.

Wormwood. Not I, Sir, I did not mind it.

Vainly. No! why some Ladies stopt their Coach, and desired to speak with me.

Vainly. Well, certainly there is not so true a Friend, nor one 10 so fit for a Confident as you are. You'll never seem to know any thing of your Friend's secrets. I do not believe if you saw me in bed with one of those Ladies, you wou'd take any Notice of it; at least, I am sure you wou'd not speak of it.

Wormwood. I am sure if I did, I shou'd not be believ'd.

Vainly. What!—You think I soar higher. No Faith, a Man in this Town must sometimes stoop below Title.

Wormwood. I'll say that for thee *Vainly*, thou hast Assurance and Pride enough to aim at an Empress.

Vainly. I vow your Complements make me blush, 'tis true, 20 tho' I have just Pride enough to keep the Best Company, and Assurance to make use of an Opportunity.

Wormwood. Mistake me not, you have however Humility
to dispense with a Kitchin Wench.

Vainly. Thou art the most agreeable Man upon Earth; you
say as obliging things to me, as I cou'd to my Mistress. But
dear *Wormwood*, dost thou really think that I can Suit my
self so handsomly to my Company? am I so very obliging,
so wondrous Civil?

30   *Wormwood.* The Civilest Person alive, for you never con-
tradicted any Man, tho' he abus'd thee, nor ever made any
Return to it but Thanks.

Vainly. Why cou'd any thing but so good a Friend, put the
Construction of Civility upon such things, if I were Guilty
of them?

Wormwood. (*Aside*) There is no freeing my self from him,
but by beating him. [*Aloud*] Look ye, Sir, I shall not be so
wondrous Civil as you are, therefore in short, neither trouble
me with your Company, nor with your professions of Friend-
40   ship.

Vainly. Why, as you say, a professing Friend is to be
suspected; we that are so Intimate, need not tell each other
that we are so.

Wormwood. We Intimate! Leave abusing me. Dost think
I wou'd be Intimate with thee? for what? for that abundance
of Powder in thy Perrewig? or for neatly Twisting that great
Slabbering Bib? or for the nice Rowl of your Stockings? or
for your Muff-String and the Buckle?

Vainly. Better and better. Why then you do think I dress
50   well; I confess all the Ladies in Town are of that Opinion.

Wormwood. (*Apart*) Abominable Rogue! [*Aloud*] I tell
thee thou dost nothing well; thou art as dull in thy Conversation, as thou art pert in thy Behaviour. You set up for
Dressing, as if you were newly return'd from *Paris*, but do it
as awkwardly as one of our Attorneys Clerks, or a young
Collegian, who has just thrown off his Gown. Thou wou'dst
be thought Brave by that Long Sword, but wou'dst fly the
sight of a Bodkin. In short, thou art in nothing what thou

wou'dst be thought, but art in every thing what thou seem'st.

Vainly. Well, such a Friend is an inestimable Jewel. I now 60
pronounce my self a happy Man in having so sincere a Friend,
so plain dealing an Acquaintance.

Wormwood. Again Friend; abuse me so again, and I'll spit
thee with thy own Sword.

Vainly. Why thou hast as much Modesty as good Nature.

Wormwood. Death, I have neither.

Vainly. Who can deal thus honestly by me; and cannot
hear your self commended with the Title of my Friend.

Wormwood. The Title of thy Friend a Commendation!
why this is past all Sufferance. Look ye, Sir, since I cannot 70
perswade you to understand me by Words, I'll try to make
you understand me by my Sword. Come, Draw Sir. (*Drawing*)

Vainly. Draw Sir?

Wormwood. Ay, draw Sir, so I say, no Repetition.

Vainly. What a Plague will you Fight a Man, because he
calls you his Friend?

Wormwood. Friend again! that word has wing'd thy
Destiny, as the Poets have it. I see the Rogue dare not Fight,
I may push this matter home.

Vainly. But Good Mr. *Wormwood.*—   80

Wormwood. Death, Sir, Draw I say, I shall make you
Dance to a New Tune.

Vainly. Oh Lard, Sir, is that all! how dull was I that I did
not understand you! I protest, dear Sir, you had reason to
take it ill, that I shou'd be so tedious in Gratifying you. I
learned a New Minuet yesterday; and tho' the place be not
so proper, yet to shew how earnest I am to oblige you. La,
La, La, La.   (*Sings and Dances*)

Wormwood. Nay, then I think I may venture to put up my
Sword, and beat Time with my Feet on your Buttocks thus 90
and thus————   [*Beats him*]

Enter Freelove *and* Bellmine.

Freelove. What, Quarrelling Gentlemen! hold, hold.

Vainly. Oh no, Sir, by no means; you do not know Mr. *Wormwood*, he's a facetious Person, and had a Mind we shou'd practice a New Dance.

Bellmine. An Antick, I suppose.

Vainly. Right, Sir, 'tis even so: if we can but get a Sett, you shall see what Sport we'll make at the next Ball.

Freelove. That, I hope, will be difficult.

100   *Wormwood.* Gentlemen, a word—I wou'd not have you seen in that little thing's Company; you see he has no Sense nor Courage, and it may make the Wise and Brave reflect on you.

Freelove. We thank you for your Caution, Sir.

Vainly. Mr. *Bellmine*, you know I always had a value for you; your Friend too seems a fine Gentleman, and I suppose is of your temper; wou'd be acceptable to the Ladies; but nothing can be so destructive to that, as being seen with that old snarling ill bred Fellow; hang him, despise him, leave him.

110   *Bellmine.* Indeed to leave him to himself, is the surest way to Plague him, for ill Nature is its own Greatest Torment.

Vainly. You are most Ingenious. Dear Mr. *Bellmine*, you and I will be wondrous great. Call your Friend away, and come with me. By your absence for some time, you may be out of Acquaintance. Come, I'll shew you every Body. I'll make you acquainted with the whole Town this Afternoon. I have access every where. You know the Ladies were always Fond of me.

Bellmine. I desire not to intermeddle between such Ladies
120   and you; therefore pray Excuse me.

Vainly. Extreamly obliging, kind to the last Degree; to deny your self so great a Pleasure, for fear of Rivaling me. But I will not suffer that so much Goodness should prejudice you. Come, we are hard by Sir *Francis Feignyouth*'s, I'll carry you thither.

Bellmine. Are you acquainted there?

Vainly. Goodness that you shou'd not know that! most intimately, Sir. Truth is, they wou'd be much fonder of me,

but I am often troubled with the Spleen, exceedingly troubled with the Spleen, Mr. *Bellmine*, and they poor Creatures do so 130 Sympathize with me, that I never go there but I give it to them.

Bellmine. Faith thou art enough to give any one the Spleen.

Vainly. Oh Good Sir, be not concern'd; I wou'd not for the world infect you; 'tis too much to be so nearly concern'd for me: Besides there is no Danger of having it in your Ingenious Company; and that is the reason I go there so often to divert it, for Sir *Francis*'s Daughter Mrs. *Marina* has a world of Wit, and her Cousin *Æmilia* is nothing short of her, they have both vast Sense, vast Sense they have indeed; and you know 140 you may depend on my Judgment. Then they Write so Charmingly.

Bellmine. Have you any of their Letters?

Vainly. Oh Goodness, Sir, what a Question is there?

Bellmine. A Question! why dost thou dare to say it?

Vainly. Not a word you say, but gives me a proof how infinitly you value me. No 'tis base to boast of a Ladies Favour, that is the truth on't. I take your Caution extream kindly Mr. *Bellmine.*

Bellmine. Death and Hell dare not to think it, not to hope 150 it, nay, not to wish it.

Vainly. Oh Enough, enough, a Word to the Wise; I will be more discreet for the future.

Bellmine. Discreet! Insolent Wretch——Death, thou deservest to be beaten.

Freelove. Bellmine so loud! Dost thou not know that next to the Disgrace of being Beaten, is that, of Beating those we know will bear it.

Bellmine. For thee even to name the Woman I admire, is almost enough to lessen my Good Opinion of her, did I not 160 know you both.

Freelove. Away, mind him not.

Vainly. Od's my Life, is one of them his Mistress? I thought there was something extraordinary it makes him so Cholerick;

he is Jealous and takes me for his Rival; nothing less cou'd
make him angry with me; But we that are admir'd by the
Women, must expect to be envied by the Men. Pox take 'em,
I cou'd bear their Envy, but I don't rellish this Quarrelling
and Striking, and Hurting and Fighting, and Wounding and
170   Dying, and the Devil and all. Where is the sense of it? I am
sure every Body is so fond of me, that if they did but know
how little I care for such things, there is not one wou'd offer
it to me, not one, I'm confident: Least these Strangers shou'd
mistake my humour, I'll march off; and there is a rare
Opportunity, a Hackney Coach coming this way with two
Masks; I'll pretend they call'd me. Heigh! you Rascal!
Coach-man, don't you hear the Ladies cry hold? Dear
Gentlemen, you see the Reason of my leaving you, there are
some Ladies in the Coach call me; therefore I hope you will
180   pardon the abrupt Departure of your most obedient faithful
Servant.   *Exit.*
   Wormwood. There's a Dog now, there's a Rogue. Why,
wou'd you prevent my Drubbing him? I wou'd have kick't
him into Jelly.
   Freelove. If you had persever'd, you had quickly made his
feeling as dull as his understanding.
   Wormwood. I attack'd his most sensible part.
   Freelove. And yet I have known some as Contemptible as
he, boast of their success in Intreagues; nay, and boast with
190   truth too, tho' one shou'd imagine that Vice alone shou'd
destroy their future Success; since it is as imprudent in Women
to put it in such Mens power to boast, as it is in the Men
base to be Guilty of it.
   Bellmine. There is none so Despicable, but have some
Quality to recommend them to some Body. Nay, it oft hap-
pens that a Man is admir'd by some, for that very Quality,
for which other despise him: And *Vainly* has one Qualification
will make many Men, and most Women value him.
   Freelove. What is that?
200   *Bellmine.* A Good Estate.

Freelove. Those who want one, imagine it to be a much greater Blessing than it is found to be by you, or any who possess it.

Wormwood. For my Part, I cannot help fretting that such dull Rogues as that, shou'd have one. 'Tis a Gift of Fortune, as much missapply'd, as to confer swiftness on the Blind; for he can make no use of it; and that is all my Comfort. He Squanders it all away in Sword, Knots, Perrewigs, Essence, Powder, and such material Things.

Freelove. Oh Sir, Let every Man dispose of his Money as   210
he pleases, so he is inoffensive to others. We have all different Appetites; his satisfaction lies in Gay Cloaths, your pleasure lies in not being pleas'd. One Man loves Drinking, another Intreagueing, *Bellmine* both; being a Man of an universal Genius.

Bellmine. Your Servant, Good Sir, you needed not have Travell'd so far for an Example. But yonder, I think, comes my old Dad that must be, who will exceed both you and I in those.

Wormwood. Yes, yes, 'tis about the Town already that you   220
are to marry his Daughter. But let me advise you one thing; Break off the Match between Sir *Francis* and my Lady *Volant*, or you will have but a slender Fortune with your Spouse.

Bellmine. But can it be possible that thou should'st give this Advice, purely out of good Nature?

Wormwood. No, I do not; mind it not; 'twill Gratifie my ill Nature, that thou shou'dst not follow good Counsel. Forward the Match, and then Marry the Daughter for pure Love. But if I were you, I wou'd chuse to Marry his Niece *Æmilia*, that   230
I might be sure not to have a Groat with her.

Freelove. And is not she a Fortune without Money?

Wormwood. Ha! ha! ha! the Man's mad. Why, what the Devil is Fortune but Money, or what is Woman or Honour or any thing else without it?

Freelove. Has she not Virtue, Sense, and Beauty?

Wormwood. The Woman is not ugly, that's the Truth on't.
But where hast thou been Educated? where hast thou spent
thy time? what hast thou convers't with? Nothing but old
240 Fables and Romances, with your *Lucretia's* and *Sempronia's*,
with your *Cassandra's* and *Clelia's*, and such stuff. In this
Age talk of Virtue and Sense! why I tell thee——
Bellmine. *Wormwood* have a care, he's the Sex's Knight
Errant.
Wormwood. Is he? (*Aside*) Why then let him suffer as much
as any of those fancy'd ones to get his Mistress, (and she prove
to be a Whore). [*To him*] But if you will not give me leave to
vent plain truths, I'll go think 'em.   *Exit.*
Freelove. I am much mistaken if this Fellow wou'd not
250 stand Kick and Cuff as heroically as t'other.
Bellmine. Altogether as rank a Poltroon; they only differ
in the manner, not in the thing. But here is one will please
us better.

Enter Sir Francis Feignyouth.

Sir *Francis.* Mr. *Bellmine*, how I rejoyce to see you again
in *Ireland*! Well, and what price bear Wine and Women now
in *London*? hah! does the *Mall* swarm with Masks, and is
French Wine admitted yet?
Bellmine. Before we talk of such weighty Affairs, let me
desire you wou'd know my Friend here.   (*Salute*)
260 Sir *Francis.* Mr. *Bellmine*, Sir, has given you a Character
will introduce you into the good opinion of all this Town.
Freelove. If it can purchase me yours, 'twill be the greatest
Service it can ever do me.
Sir *Francis.* Oh Sir, your own Merit will always give you
an absolute sway over, Sir, your most faithful humble Servant.
Freelove. My Merit, Sir, will make but a slender Figure in
the presence of so accomplish'd a Person as Sir *Francis
Feignyouth.*
Sir *Francis.* I protest, Sir, you make me blush—Nay no
270 more I beseech you, my modesty will not suffer you to proceed.

(*Apart*) An exceeding well-bred ingenious Person!

Bellmine. (*Apart*) So, he has won his heart already.

Sir Francis. Mr. *Bellmine*, no one has a better taste of Man than you. You have done your Country Service by bringing so fine a Gentleman to it. May I crave your Name, Sir?

Freelove. *Freelove*, at your Service, Sir.

Sir Francis. I have known several of that Name in *England*, fine Gentlemen all. Well, Sir, for your comfort, you will find Women here that are not Despicable; I know 'tis the greatest Commendation of any place to you young Gentlemen; But then Opportunities are scarce, there's no getting at 'em. 　280

Bellmine. I hope that is no Fault to you who have a Family, Sir *Francis*?

Sir Francis. No, no, I speak in reference to you Gentlemen; I am past such things my self.

Freelove. Past it, Sir! a Man of your Make, your Health and Sanguine Constitution, past it! no Sir, you are as Vigorous as ever.

Sir Francis. Think you so, Mr. *Freelove*? Do I seem very Strong, very Sanguine, very Vigorous? hah! 　290

Freelove. As Five and Twenty, Sir.

Sir Francis. You Flatter me; I shou'd find it hard to perswade the Women to that Belief.

Freelove. No Woman that has Eyes in her Head will doubt it; if she does, you can convince her another way.

Sir Francis. Ods me, I'll go see my Mistress incontinently: I am not so decay'd as I thought. Well, Mr. *Freelove*, I am much oblig'd to you for your Complements; if you will meet me at the Coffee-House this Evening, I'll carry you to see my Mistress, to receive your Sentiments of her. I have a great 　300 Relyance on your Judgment; so much, that since you think me fit for it, I am resolv'd to be Marry'd to Morrow.

Bellmine. How Sir! to be Marry'd!

Sir Francis. Ay, to be Marry'd, Sir, what have you to say against that Holy State? you will not declaim against Marriage before me, I hope?

Bellmine. By no means, Sir, since I admire your Daughter, you may be sure it is that I covet.

310 *Sir Francis.* Do you so, then why do you not Marry, if you like one another?

Bellmine. I can promise for my self, and I hope there is no Aversion on her side. But there is something else to be Considered.

Sir Francis. What than Love! Do you pretend to Love, and Consider any thing else but Love? Consider! pish, that word agrees as ill with Love, as with one of thy age. Why, when I was a young Fellow, I never consider'd any thing but how to get a Mistress, and then how to get rid of her.

Bellmine. But you know, Sir *Francis*, in Matrimonial Cases,
320 we are to consider how to maintain Children, and House-keeping, and a Wife will expect a Coach, and a fine Equipage, and Gay Cloaths, and——

Sir Francis. And the Devil and all, I know it Sir, I know it.

Bellmine. Now Sir, tho' I have a tolerable Estate, yet the better to support your Daughter's Grandeur——

Sir Francis. You wou'd have me starve my self.

Bellmine. No, no, I shall be very Moderate.

Sir Francis. Phoo, trust to my Fatherly Love Boy, trust to that. If not, yonder she goes; look upon her, and Consider if you can.

330 *Bellmine.* Is that she Sir? *(Aside)* *Freelove*, the very Two we have been talking with this Morning! what a couple of Dull Rogues were we?

Sir Francis. Is that she? you a Lover, and can't distinguish your Mistress in a Mask! Yes, 'tis she, and my fine Niece *Æmilia*. Talk of Portions! Look on 'em I say; there's a Motion, there's an Air, there's an Air: See, see, how firm they tread, hah? and then see their Hips, how they jut, how they rowl. Go, get ye gone, ye lazy Fellows, get ye gone. Ods me, don't stand staring after them, but follow them, and try
340 how our Ladies can talk. Go, get ye gone. *Exit Bellmine.*

Freelove. Well Sir, I'll meet you at the Coffee-House.

Exit Freelove.

Sir Francis. Very well, away, away.
These young Fellows now adays are perfectly of the Womens
temper, must be forc'd to do what they Languish for, or they
keep themselves so low, they must take time to be rais'd; I
believe I am brisker than any of them——How the Jades
have fir'd me. Wou'd I cou'd meet with any thing that were
not my own Flesh and Blood now——Any thing tho' she
were in a Stuff Riding-hood.

> *We that have Vigour, and our Stomachs keen,*   350
> *Can eat of any Dish, that's sound and clean.*   *Exit.*

Enter Marina *followed by* Bellmine.

Bellmine. Now am I resolv'd, for once, to give her a small
proof of my unshaken Fidelity.
Marina. Now cannot I find in my heart to discover my self,
tho' I long he shou'd know me. I see, to Deceive is a greater
Pleasure to our Sex, than to Love.
Bellmine. I perceive you are a Woman of Honour, by being
so punctual to your assignation; but I am sorry so much
Kindness as well as Justice, is thrown away on a Man, who is
not inclinable to make use of either.   360
Marina. So indifferent, Sir! you talk't in another strain this
Morning.
Bellmine. Then I had some Reasons.
Marina. Why do you not still?
Bellmine. The Cause is remov'd.
Marina. What was that?
Bellmine. To give my Friend an Opportunity to talk to
yours.
Marina. Why do you follow me now?
Bellmine. To contradict what I then said.   370
Marina. Truly, Sir, 'tis a very needless Trouble you give
your self, for be assur'd, I as little valu'd, as I credited what
you said.
Bellmine. You see however, I am a Man of Conscience, and
cou'd not rest satisfied, till I endeavour'd to convince you——

Marina. How little you value me.

Bellmine. That I value you——as much as a prudent Man ought to do a Mask. But that the Fates have otherwise dispos'd of my Heart.

380 *Marina.* Oh Ridiculous! is the Creature in Love!

Bellmine. Ridiculous?

Marina. Do not you know that every particular Woman despises a Man for Loving any thing but her dear Self? and will you be contemn'd by the whole Sex, to be esteem'd by one?

Bellmine. I very well know, Madam, Love is a Passion despis'd by all over whom it has not a present Sway; not only by those who never yet Lov'd, but even by those who have Lov'd. But I never make other Men's sentiments a standard

390 for my Pleasures.

Marina. And will you be laugh'd at by your own Sex, and despis'd by ours? and all perhaps for one who Loves some body else; Nay, 'tis very likely for one of so little Wit, that you will be laugh'd at more for your choice than passion.

Bellmine. Nothing can justify the Excess of my Passion, but the Excellence of the Object.

Marina. I have known some doat even on Deformity, and say the same thing; have fancy'd Beauties where there was nothing but Faults. But for my part, I shou'd think it a

400 scurvy Complement to have my Lover say, his Passion and my Beauties, were owing to his Fancy.

Bellmine. And yet the most perfect owe their Conquests to that, or we shou'd all Love the same Person.

Marina. I doubt not but your Fancy is unrivall'd. Some Nauceous thing.

Bellmine. I tell thee perverse Woman, she is the most excellent of her kind; she is beyond my description; not only beyond your belief, but imagination.

Marina. Fulsom.

410 *Bellmine.* Thou dost almost provoke me to treat thee roughly; but that I perceive something in thy Air and Shape,

not much different from hers, and for which I honour you.

Marina. Alas poor Dissembler! I thought I shou'd Discover whence this uncommon Fidelity of yours proceeded. You very well knew to whom you profess'd it, and to whom you address'd these Commendations. I do not doubt but the old Gentleman I saw you talk to, discover'd to you, who your humble Servant was.   (*Unmasks*)

Bellmine. Bless me, Madam, is it you!

How cou'd you have the Conscience to tempt Humane   420
Frailty thus? and wou'd you have blam'd me, if I had been false to you, when tempted by you?

Marina. As if you did not know me!

Bellmine. Know you! impossible. Come, indeed I shou'd chide you, as well for trying my Faith, as for concealing your self so long, when you know the Business of my coming here was to see you, and the Business of my Life to serve you. When I am sensible of no pleasure without you, and have no wish beyound you.

Marina. Hold, hold, or I shall believe you imagine I have   430
my Mask on still; when nothing will pass for good Sense that is not strain'd beyond it; nor for a Complement under Profaneness; nor for Love that is not ridiculously affected.

Bellmine. You must allow a little heat at first sight, after so tedious an Absence.

Marina. That shall not excuse you, if I find you knew me, for I cannot endure to be undermin'd.

Bellmine. What will convince you that I did not? shall I have recourse to Swearing? and——

Marina. And Dissembling. No, those are too oft practis'd   440
to gain Credit with me. But come, I'll refer it to your Friend that is walking before us; I hear he's a Man of Sincerity: And if you have fool'd me, by talking thus, when you all the time knew me, expect nothing but Frowns from me these three Days.   *Exeunt.*

Enter Æmilia follow'd by Freelove.

Freelove. (*Speaks entring Aside*) I will still pretend I know her not, that I may see how she will resent my Passion for another.

[*To her*] Believe me, Madam, when I protest it was an
450 affected, and own it was a brutal Entertainment you receiv'd from me this Morning. But I come now full of Repentance, and full of Hopes you entertain the same favourable Thoughts of me, you then seem'd to have.

Æmilia. There has no alteration happen'd in my Mind since, but there seems to be in yours.

Freelove. A Reflection on your Goodness, Wit, Shape, and Air, was able to soften a heart more hard than mine; But a second View and farther Proofs, have confirm'd it to you.

Æmilia (*Aside*) Shou'd he say this and not know me? I'm
460 lost. [*To him*] A bad Face (as perhaps mine is) will soon lose my Conquest.

Freelove. It must be bad indeed, if so many other Charms cannot attone for it. Be what it will, I admire it.

Æmilia. You prove your Generosity in giving your heart to a Stranger; but that makes me doubt your Constancy; a Virtue in a Lover, which every Woman has the Vanity to expect, tho' so few deserve it.

Freelove. You want no assurances of my future Constancy, if you believe I now Love you; for no one ever Lov'd, who
470 did not conclude he shou'd always Love the same.

Æmilia. I must conclude you very Rash and Imprudent, to profess such Love to you know not whom.

Freelove. The more I shew my Imprudence, the fiercer I prove my flame; trust me, it is a Dull and Languid Passion, which can be check'd by any Consideration. Shall I, to be thought prudent by a World, where some will hate me for being so, and the rest do me no good, debar my self of real Pleasures? No, no, Prudence must submit to pleasure, with me.

Æmilia. What! have you no regard to Reputation?
480 *Freelove.* As much as any Man. But whatever we pretend 'tis pleasure rules us. We do not this, nor forbear that, for the

real good of the thing, but that it pleases us. The Woman that is Chast, is not so for the sake of that Virtue, but the Fame of being so, delights her more, than the Joys she receives by being otherwise. When any Woman refuses what I request, and Love prompts; I conclude, 'tis because she values something more than Love and me; and she who suffers any thing to come in Competition with her Love, Loves not.

Æmilia. You have given me great Advantage over you; for since I have not profess'd a Passion for you, I am not oblig'd   490
to any of these Extravagancies, but you are.

Freelove. I own it. There is nothing I will refuse, that Love and you require.

Æmilia. And you profess this mighty Passion to me only?

Freelove. Witness it Heaven and Earth, to you only.

Æmilia. Ungrateful Fickle Man! [*Unmasking*] Look here, behold this Face, and be as much confounded to behold who 'tis, as grieved 'tis not a Stranger to your Baseness.——Oh that Submission well becomes thee now, but dost thou think I am that same forgiving Fool, a Bow can Reconcile me to   500
thee, make me forget thy inconsiderate Rash Temper? when e're I do, I shall forget thee too; remembring one, I shall remember both, and both despise.

Freelove. 'Tis as I wish'd.

Æmilia. What's as you wish'd? that I have found thee false; art thou come here only to publish it? 'tis well thou canst not publish too, that I ever made thee a Return to thy feign'd Passion; that wou'd indeed encrease thy Pride.

Freelove. You never have till now.

Æmilia. Till now! unheard of Impudence! what! when I   510
tell how I disdain a Vice, must you misconstrue it for Love?

Freelove. Yet, am I pleas'd, o'rejoy'd at all this Wrath, which shews your Jealousy; the greatest sign I e're cou'd yet receive, that I am not indifferent to you; to have this proof it was, that I disguis'd my knowledge who you were.

Æmilia. Oh Hypocrite! Artful Dissembler! how quick to catch at an Excuse! this shews thy Cunning, not thy Innocence, while I suppos'd thee Honest, 'twas easy to delude me, and gain a Credit in every thing. Now thou art known, I doubt each word. Even known Truths utter'd by thee, wou'd be suspected.

Freelove. Do not Persist in this; why will you dash my rising Joy, my first and only hour of Bliss? I sought to know if you valu'd me enough to be Jealous, and wou'd be happy in the search, cou'd I now remove your Doubts——for I Love——

Æmilia. No doubt, you Love; Love every thing you meet; and therefore 'tis I'll none of it. Therefore I'll leave you to gratify your Roving Humour. Run, Fawn, Caress each Common Thing you meet; give them thy heart, a present only fit for such; try which can affect a Passion most, and which can first Deceive. While such as I, look with disdain on thee, and pity upon them.　　　　　　　　　　*Exit.*

Freelove. Oh Confusion! what have I done? searching to discover her Love, my only Happiness, I have forfeited it. Curse on my impertinent Curiosity.

Enter Bellmine.

Curse on my dull Designs! my Concern too hindred my telling her, her Uncle cou'd witness I knew her. Before she's undeceiv'd, she may take some resolution for ever Fatal to my Love and Quiet. Nay, I have given her a Moments disquiet; were I an Age upon a Rack, 'twere but a poor Attonement. Oh, I cou'd tear this prating Tongue out by the Roots, beat out these stupid Brains; and only spare my heart, because 'tis hers.

Bellmine. What's the meaning of all this? here's some Mischief towards. I met your Mistress frowning, and find you ranting. What Quarrel already! this Matrimony runs so in your head, it has quite spoil'd your Humour; stay till the Comfortable indissolvable Knot is ty'd, and then I shan't wonder. You Jarr like Man and Wife already.

Freelove. Oh *Bellmine!* I have done the most imprudent

thing—You need not wonder at my Rage, since you beheld
her frowns. I am the Ridiculous Cause of Both. I must be
making Experiments.

Bellmine. Why, I have been about some such matter too,
which had like to have happen'd ill. But thanks to a little
decent Assurance, and some few necessary Oaths, all's well
again. My fair Lady having no great reason to think me the
most constant of Lovers, I was resolv'd to let her see, I was
not to be tempted, and pretended not to know her.   560

Freelove. Did you leave her in that Opinion?

Bellmine. Or I would ne're have left her. I were a hopeful
Fellow indeed, and had improv'd my Time well in the world,
if I cou'd not perswade and swear my Mistress to any Opinion.

Freelove. You swore it too, you did not know her?

Bellmine. Swore it! ay lustily: what dost think I wou'd
scruple an Oath to put a Lady in a good Humour?

Freelove. What unlucky Stars were they which brought us
together, and what an unnatural Conjunction; that ever I
should enter into strict Friendship with one who is my perfect   570
Reverse!

Bellmine. What art thou mad?

Freelove. I Dreaded I had ruin'd my self, and you have
Conscientiously by your Genteel Qualities of Lying and
Swearing confirm'd it. I am undone, if *Æmilia* believes I did
not know her, and *Marina* will confirm her in that belief,
thanks to your Industry and Conscience.

Bellmine. Pish is that all? why, I'll forswear it again, Man,
to do you Service.

Freelove. If you cou'd but prevail with your self to speak   580
truth, there wou'd be no occasion for this Complaisance.

Bellmine. Speak truth to a Woman! why you see what
comes of it. I tell thee the Sex bear such a Detestation to it,
that no man ever succeeded with them that practis'd it. But
come, Sir *Francis Feignyouth* expects us by this time to carry
us a visiting; I have a mind to see whither her Ladyship be
improv'd in Scandal; what new Reputations she has sacrific'd

to her Malice.

Freelove. I am in no humour to be delighted with such
590 things.

Bellmine. I never knew any Man so easily dejected in Love
Affairs. I have already advis'd you always to dissemble in
Relation to Women. I will give you one Caution more, in
relation to all matters as well as to that.

> Ne're let your mind be with Despair o'recast;
> But always hope, you will Succeed at last.
> 'Tis better far to hope, altho' those hopes deceive,
> Than to despair of Bliss, and yet the Bliss receive.

Exeunt.

ACT III

Scene Lady Volant's.

Enter Timothy *and Lady* Volant.

Timothy. DON'T you think, Madam, that I'll bear this Life any longer, I will not endure to be us'd thus; nor must you think to talk to me at this Rate.

Lady Volant. Not suffer me to talk! you sawcy Fellow; do you know who I am?

Timothy. A very needless Question to be put to me by my Lady *Volant*, considering the Familiarities that have past between us; your Pride, your Malice, your Inquisitiveness, your Detraction, are known to all the Town; and your Lady- ships Chastity and Wealth in a more particular manner to your pretended Steward, *Timothy Tellpenny.*

Lady Volant. And do you upbraid me for having these Qualities so agreeable to your self; and for the want of those you have ruin'd? Did I take you up half Starv'd, and in Rags, Fed you like an Epicure, and Cloath'd you like a Gentleman, till you are as overgrown in Bulk, as with Pride? maintain'd you so well, made you live in so much Plenty and Ease, that there is as great an alteration in your Person as Circum- stances; so great, that you neither are known by others nor by your self: And is this the Reward I have?

Timothy. No, you have been rewarded to the full, my Good Lady. That you nourish'd my Person, was for your own sake;

if I had not been of more than Herculean strength, you had
reduc'd me to a Shadow e're this, to ashes. And has not the
Credit of my being your Steward gain'd you so much? Have
not I manag'd and spar'd prudently, and borrow'd for you
profusely? Have not I by my Art impos'd you on the Town
for a great Fortune, when you know you were never able to
give me a Guinea, that I did not first borrow for you?

30 Lady *Volant*. But who must pay those Debts?

 Timothy. Who? my Wit must; your Jointure never will.
Have not I wrought Sir *Francis Feignyouth* to Love you?
Have not I perswaded him to a Belief, that your ill Nature
is Wit, and that your Pride is Virtue; that the decay of your
Person proceeds from a neglect of your self, and not from
Age; tho' you know you are equally industrious to be thought
handsome your self, as that no body else may be thought so.
And have not I made your Poverty pass upon him for good
Management? and least we shou'd be disappointed of him,

40 have I not us'd the same Arts to *Vainly*?

 Lady *Volant*. You have taken Pains to get me a Husband,
that I must own.

 Timothy. As much as ever a young sanguine Wife did, to
get an Heir to a Rich feeble Husband; gone to as many
places, and try'd as many Men.

 Lady *Volant*. But to what purpose have you succeeded yet?

 Timothy. Ay, to be sure 'tis the Man is always blameable.
I had succeeded long since, if you wou'd be pleas'd to govern
that unruly Member, your Tongue; which is ever employ'd

50 in Flattering the present, and Railing at the absent; so dis-
oblige both; for so you do but rail, you no more consider to
whom, than of whom you speak.

 Lady *Volant*. Nay, Good *Tim*, I relent, thy words pierce
my heart.

 Timothy. You will exclaim against a standing Army before
a broken Officer, and praise one before a politick Senator;
you are never of the same Religion with those you are in
Company with, but change it with every Visitor: A Fanatick

before Papists, and with Fanaticks for *Jure divino*; you
commend *Ireland* when out of it, and abominate it now you   60
are here; you condemn Plays before Poets, and adore Sermons
before Atheists; you rail at Ladies before their Lovers; and at
Husbands before their Wives; but that I think is not much
minded, you have not got many Enemies by that.

Lady *Volant.* I beseech you, do not treat me thus.

Timothy. Is there one Person in Town you have not vili-
fied? and to make the Scandal bring more certain Ruin with
it, have you not aspers'd other people with your own actions?
Do I not know all your Faults, and have not I carefully conceal'd all for above these three years, that I have known you?   70

Lady *Volant.* Thou hast, I own it, I was to blame to deny
thee.

Timothy. And after all I have done, and all I expect to do,
refuse me a Guinea, and when I carry'd the Plate to pawn too.

Lady *Volant.* There, there's a couple for you, tho' you know
dear *Tim,* how very few more I have left.

Timothy. Pretty Rogues! Comfortable Rogues! how they
mollify me! how they smile on me! you know Madam, [this]
is to carry on your Projects, alas, what occasion shou'd I have
for Money, but to do you Service! what have I almost forgot!   80
Mr. *Bellmine,* who they say is to Marry *Sir Francis's* Daughter,
is Landed this Morning; now you must use all your Art to
delay this Marriage, till your own be perfected, and till you
have got the Knights Money in your own hands; for Mr.
Bellmine, having a good Estate, will require a great Portion,
which will disable Sir *Francis* from paying your Debts, and
spoil our Projects on him, for his Estate being Entail'd, he
cannot raise much, and the moment he is Married, I will
arrest him for Four or Five thousand Pounds you must pretend to owe me.   90

Lady *Volant.* Four or Five thousand! Ten or Twelve.

Timothy. Ever insatiable. No, no, such a Debt and the
Bondage of Matrimony together, will break his heart.

Lady *Volant.* Well, I leave all to your Management.

Timothy. Is not that a Coach stopt? 'tis some visitor, I will
usher them up.   *Exit.*
Lady *Volant.* How insolent the Rogue is grown! Thus we
are ever us'd by such Fellows, when we put our selves in their
Power; and we never treat them better than they deserve, but
100 they treat us as we deserve; I am glad however he knows not
my Grand Secret; that wou'd make him Ten times more
sawcy. I have conceal'd it above these five years, not only
from him, but from the whole Town, and with much ado,
heaven knows, considering how much depends on it, the
place, and my Female Frailties, for I have observ'd that
Secrets of the greatest Consequence, are preserv'd with the
greatest pain. That we cou'd but keep a Sercet with as much
ease, as we can dissemble! but the Reason's plain, the one
gives us trouble, the other pleasure, as for Example.

Enter Vainly.

110 Mr. *Vainly*, your most humble Servant.
Vainly. Your most Obedient Vassal, Dear Madam.
Lady *Volant.* Your Company, Mr. *Vainly*, is so coveted by
every one, that it is impossible you shou'd make any parti-
cular person happy with it, often or long. You are grown a
Stranger here.
Vainly. I protest Madam, ever since I was here last night,
I have been so tormented with the Spleen.
Lady *Volant.* Alas Sir, that is a cruel Distemper truly. But
it is a Fine you must pay for Wit. You Wits are all subject
120 to that.
Vainly. We are so indeed, Madam; and really I believe I
have it to a more violent degree than any one. I swear
Madam, it has such an effect on me sometimes, that I do
not put above half a pound of Powder in my Perriwig for a
whole day, and [it] Discomposes my Face so violently, that I
cannot bear even the sight of a Looking-Glass, and I hurry
abroad without the Garniture of a Patch, or a Sword-knot.
Lady *Volant.* Is't possible! nay, if it makes you neglect your

self, your Friends must expect to be serv'd so too.

Vainly. Every thing is disagreeable to me then, but your   130
Ladyship. (*Aside*) That I think was Nice.

Lady *Volant.* Oh Lard, Sir!

Vainly. Nay, I swear 'tis truth. Alas Madam, 'tis scarce a
Complement in this dull Town.

Lady *Volant.* Do you think it so too, Mr. *Vainly?*

Vainly. Oh Madam, I cannot bear it.

Lady *Vol.* Nay solemnly, Sir, it was a great while before I
cou'd; it agreed as ill with my Constitution, as it doth with
my Inclinations; but, thank my Stars, I have done tolerably
well, since my being *Naturaliz'd.* How fortunate am I to have   140
my Opinion strengthen'd by one of your Judgment! 'tis ?
horrid place, and I vow (as you say Mr. *Vainly*) I do not see
a pretty Woman in it.

Vainly. Not one but your Ladyship; nor is there an agreeable Man here.

Lady *Volant.* Only Mr. *Vainly.* The Women are so affected.

Vainly. And the Men so Proud.

Lady *Volant.* So Censorious——

Vainly. And so selfish—and when a parcel of 'em are met
together, so talkative.   150

Lady *Volant.* They make as much Noise as a Crowd of
Apprentices at a Bonfire.

Vainly. But now we talk of such People; Mr. *Bellmine* is
Landed this Morning, who is to Marry Mrs. *Marina;* and
with him there is come a Gentleman who has the same design
on *Æmilia.*

Lady *Volant.* No doubt they'll succeed; since one is as little
admir'd for her Wit and Beauty, as the other is for her
Fortune.

Vainly. Ha, ha, ha, Your Ladyship has the neatest Way of   160
Railery. I have had some Encouragements there; and I do not
doubt but Mr. *Freelove* (for that's his Name) will desist as I
did, when she hears he is a Beggar, and when he has seen your
Ladyship.

Lady *Volant*. You are so obliging—But pray what sort of a Man is he? he must needs be an extraordinary Person who has so particular a Fancy.

Vainly. He was very fond of me, till he began to suspect me for his Rival, so was *Bellmine* too. The best I know of him
170 is, he is just come from dear *England*, and has been lately in much dearer *France*. The worst I know of him, or indeed can know is, that tho' he wears fine Cloaths, he has no more Money than his Mistress.

Lady *Volant*. Oh hideous!

Vainly. The best Jest is (for all the Town know it already) tho' they are acquainted with each other's Condition, they are in Love with each other, and are resolv'd to Marry.

Lady *Volant*. And Starve. Oh Matrimony and Poverty join'd, are Comfortable Things! Sure his Head is as empty
180 as his Pocket.

Vainly. That I suppose, you will soon be convinc'd of; for I saw him with Sir *Francis Feignyouth*, who I do not Question will bring him here this Evening.

Lady *Volant*. Alas, Mr. *Vainly*, you know I cannot be so rude to refuse a Visit, or I wou'd never suffer that Ridiculous Fellow to come within my Doors; but Civility often constrains us to do what we hate.——I think I hear some Body coming ——You'll pardon me if I retire, it wou'd not bear the appearance of Decency to be found Entertaining you alone;
190 I assure you my Woman wou'd not behave her self thus, were any other here but you. You'll Excuse me Sir——

Vainly. Oh Dear Madam, this Confidence in me, is the greatest Honour that can be conferr'd on, Madam, your most Obedient Servant.   *Exit Lady* Volant.

She is fond of me to a violent Degree, that's plain; the next time I come, I will propose Marriage to her; I fear no Rival, especially that Old Fopp.

Enter Sir Francis Feignyouth, Freelove *and* Bellmine.

Sir *Francis*. Come Gentlemen, come, you shall see now, if

I han't made a Good Choice, you shall.——Ha! how! what!
Vainly here! Pray Sir, if I may be so bold, what is your   200
Business here?

Vainly. My Business, Sir!

Sir *Francis.* Ay Sir, your Business, Sir; I think I speak very
plain, Sir?

Vainly. Oh Dear Sir *Francis*! Plain Dealing is a Jewel, you
cannot oblige me more, than to deal plainly and freely by me.
I take it for a signal proof of your Kindness.

Sir *Francis.* Here's a shifting young Rogue; who wou'd
have thought it had so much Cunning. But answer me to the
purpose, or I shall try how you can evade a Pass of this. What   210
is your Business here?

Vainly. The Business of all the World, Sir; to wait on my
Lady *Volant.*

Sir *Francis.* Is it so? And have you seen her?

Vainly. Have I seen her! Oh Goodness, what a Question
there is? Pray Sir, do my Visits use to be refus'd, Sir?

Sir *Francis.* There are indeed some Ladies, who treat all
Men alike, the Impertinent with the same Regard they do the
Man of Sense, the Little, Fidling, Prating Fop like the Man of
Honour and Discretion; But my Lady *Volant* is no such, she   220
can distinguish, she can Sir——

Vainly. Ay, I know it Sir, I know it; and you will find so in
a little time.

Sir *Francis.* Why ye Little, Young Pert, Prating, Fidling
Boaster, do you hope to Succeed, where I have Pretensions?
Don't you know that I can Fight? ha——

Freelove. Not with this Gentleman I hope, Sir *Francis.*
Methinks you mistake the right use of him; he is properer for
your Diversion than your Anger.

Vainly. Ay Sir, 'tis very true. I have fought, Sir, several   230
times, but in my Opinion, Laughing and Talking is better
Sport by the half.

Bellmine. Especially to one whom it becomes so well as you.

Vainly. Your most humble Servant, Sir: I am glad we have

Gentlemen come to us now that understand Breeding and
Conversation; 'Tis not to be had here. I protest, Sir, I am
forced to go to *England* once a year, to refine my understanding.

Bellmine. What need you put your self to that Trouble?
240   Cannot you keep a Correspondence with your Taylor?

Vainly. With my Taylor, Sir?

Bellmine. Yes; For all you Learn by your Journey, is a New
Fashion; and all you understand is, whither your Cloaths be
well made.

Vainly. You are so obliging, Sir. Truly I think this Coat
is very well Cut, fits with a Good Air. I had it sent me by an
Express from *London*; for I cannot bear any thing but what
comes from thence. Oh 'tis a happy Place! and in a blessed
Country, where there are all things necessary, where there
250   are such pleasures, and such Conveniencies to enjoy them!

Freelove. I have been told you have all those here.

Vainly. Oh not one, Sir, not one.

Freelove. You have good Wine?

Vainly. Yes, yes, that's true, I had forgot that.

Freelove. Plenty of all sorts of Fish and Flesh.

Vainly. Phoo, they are perfect Drugs. Plenty of Meat and
Drink; but nothing else.

Freelove. The People are Civil and Obliging.

Vainly. Especially to Strangers.
260   *Freelove.* And Hospitable.

Vainly. To a Fault, Sir.

Freelove. The Air is Good, a temperate Climate.

Vainly. Much the same as in *England*.

Freelove. The Soil is Rich.

Vainly. Oh 'tis too Rank.

Freelove. What necessaries then, or what pleasures do you
want? You have fine Women.

Vainly. They are kind I am sure.

Freelove. To you chiefly I suppose.
270   *Vainly.* Shall I make a Confession then among my Friends?

I do not believe ever any Man has been so successful. I do not know that ever I ask'd in vain.

Sir *Francis*. I can hold no longer. Why thou little worthless Contemptible Wretch! Do you entertain Strangers with your aversion for your Country, without being able to give one Reason for it; and can you give but one Reason for liking it, which if it were true, would make all others abhor it? The Women fond of thee! Why the Common Hackneys who live by thee, Contemn thee. But such as he think if he is not affronted, he is belov'd.   280

Vainly. You must know, Sir, (*to* Freelove) he is Jealous of me, that makes him so peevish, he us'd to be very fond of me. Therefore I'll tell you more of this some other time, and in the mean time study all Opportunities of shewing how much I am, Sir, Your most Obedient humble Servant.   *Exit.*

Freelove. Your Servant Sir. This Spark takes leave, I perceive, always alike, I suppose too of every Body alike, and in the same Stile as he concludes his dull Insipid Billet-doux.

Sir *Francis*. Ay, hang him, hang him, he is always dully Brisk and Impertinent. But here she comes who is all per- 290 fection.

Enter Lady Volant.

Madam, Your Ladyships Slave. Be pleas'd to know these Two Gentlemen; this is Mr. *Freelove*, and this is Mr. *Bellmine*. You see, Madam, how Communicative I am to you of every thing that is Good; you shall share all my Goods.

Lady *Volant*. This is a signal Proof indeed.

Sir *Francis*. This Gentleman is in Love with my Niece, and this with my Daughter. What say you, Madam, shall we be Married all together? keep time, odd, I believe I cou'd— make it a day of Revelling, and a night of Loving, Feast all 300 day and Kiss all night.

Lady *Volant*. Sir *Francis*, I have all the Respect and Friendship for you, that a Man of your Excellent Parts can require with Modesty, but I must desire you not to talk so loosly before me. Marriage is a sacred thing, Sir *Francis*, a very sacred thing; yet it is a thing, Sir *Francis*, that may be abus'd, and may be perverted to raise indecent and unruly Cogitations.

Sir *Francis*. (*To* Freelove *and* Bellmine) I told you how reserv'd she was.

310   Lady *Volant*. I presume you found Mr. *Vainly* here. I assure you, Sir *Francis*, I left the Room because he tacitly imply'd the thing Marriage, tho' on his knees, and with all the Chastity and Modesty imaginable.

Bellmine. (*To* Freelove) There she has given the Reason.

Freelove. Can he mistake this for Virtue? I wou'd as soon take a Bully's Rant for true Courage, or a Cringing Designing Courtiers low bow for true Humility. This Ridiculous Cant, this affected Squeamishness is as nauseous to me, as open Lewdness, and I am sure as certain a sign, and a greater

320   Crime, for she adds Hypocrisy.

Bellmine. I am so far of your Opinion, that if you will take him aside, I am resolv'd to make Love to her.

Freelove. What at first! and to what end?

Bellmine. I have just now a Project conceiv'd in my head, but I have not time now to impart it.

Sir *Francis*. Son *Bellmine*, you must try to prevail with my Lady here, and as you succeed with her for me, so you must expect to succeed with me for my Daughter.

Lady *Volant* (*Aside*) Oh for some Art to Charm him from

330   *Marina*; or at least delay the Match; for I must dally no longer with my old Gentleman.

Bellmine. This is a severe Task, Madam, that Sir *Francis* has impos'd upon me : To require me to make Love to you, and not for my self.

Lady *Volant*. He is very sensible, Sir, that his Daughter has Charms to secure you from one much more engaging.

Bellmine. Fathers are as Blind as Lovers. And give me leave to think he is a much more indulgent Father, than passionate Lover, or he wou'd dread your greater Power wou'd make me

340   false both to my Love and Friendship : And shou'd *Marina*

make the same Tryal of my Constancy, she wou'd convince me
she exceeds you as much in Vanity, as she is inferiour to you
in every Charm.

Lady Volant. Truly, Sir, if Sir *Francis* had such a Talent of
Elocution, I believe he might have succeeded long since. And
for his Daughter, I conjecture I am not much inferiour to her
in the superlative Charm, Fortune.

Bellmine. That never was a Charm to me; tho' I cou'd wish
it were one to you, since I can at least equal Sir *Francis*'s.

Lady Volant. Sure, Sir, you can have no other design in   350
this, but to try with what temper I can support such Complements.

Bellmine. That is not my design, I assure you.

Lady Volant. Is it not indeed, Sir? on your Veracity.

Bellmine. No, on my Honour, Madam; nor can you suppose
it is. Methinks a Lady of your piercing Wit, shou'd in a
Moment read ones thoughts, as in a Moment so much Beauty
Conquers.

Lady Volant. 'Tis as dangerous to believe one of you young
Gentlemen, as it is difficult to deny so fine a Person.   360

Bellmine. Convince me, you think me the latter, by allowing
me a Moments Free Conversation.

Lady Volant. Alas Sir, even to talk thus is a Liberty I never
permitted to any before; and I am sure you cannot in reason
ask more.

Bellmine. Lovers are always thought Extravagant in their
Demands, by the indifferent. Therefore I fear to ask what I
wou'd give the World for, that you wou'd let me see you this
Evening in St. *Stephen*'s-*Green*.

Lady Volant. Oh me Sir, what wou'd the World say! or   370
what I value more, what wou'd you think?

Bellmine. The World shall never know it, and for me——

[They go aside]

Sir Francis. What say you Sir, have you no Estate?

Freelove. Not an Acre, Sir.

Sir Francis. Nor Money?

Freelove. Not a Penny.

Sir *Francis* (*Aside*) A strange dull Fellow this! [*To him*]
And have you really now the Conscience to make Love to
my Niece? Can you imagine that she will throw her self away
380 upon you in the Bloom of her Youth; one of her Wit and
Beauty? But perhaps you think she has an Equal Stock of
Money, and so hope to make your Fortune by her : But I can
assure you, she is in the same Circumstances as you are, not
worth a Penny.

Freelove. I knew it when first I saw her, yet my Love
receiv'd not the least Check by that; I hope she will prove
as Generous.

Sir *Francis.* Generous do you call it? Death! you make me
mad. What a Pox is there no way to be thought Generous,
390 but by becoming Mad and Begging. And pray Sir, if I may
ask you a Civil Question, if she were Generous enough, as you
call it, and mad enough, as I call it, to Marry you, how wou'd
you Maintain her, Sir?

Freelove. Oh, trust to our Stars for that.

Sir *Francis.* I hope she will have more Grace. Trust to your
Stars for that! I wou'd as soon trust you for ten Thousand
Pounds. (*Aside*) I have not heard a Fellow talk so Sillily in all
my life.

Freelove. And I assure you Sir, were our Circumstances
400 chang'd, you shou'd command that Summ from me. I have
so great an Honour for you, and so high an Opinion of your
Worth and Integrity.

Sir *Francis.* (*Aside*) Strangely Impertinent! [*To him*] I
beseech you good Romantick Sir, put not your self to the
trouble of making these professions to me, for to be free with
you, I no more regard your Complements than I want your
assistance. (*Aside*) A Perfect Fool! Methinks too a very ugly,
ungentile Man, as ever I saw!

Freelove. I hope, Sir, I shall not find you my Enemy in this
410 matter however.

Sir *Francis.* No, no Sir, you need no other Enemy than

your self, and those Stars you were talking of. Your Servant Sir, I must mind my own Affairs now. (*Aside*) What a confounded Friend has *Bellmine* chosen out? no doubt a Sharper, and lives upon him. But I'll quickly part 'em, when he is Married to my Daughter.

Freelove. (*Aside*) 'Tis well my Breach with *Æmilia* is repaired, by his owning he told me who she was, or he wou'd never do me that Justice now; for I perceive by this Declaration of mine, I have forfeited his good Opinion. He cannot   420 relish even Flattery from the mouth of a Man he thinks is in want.

Sir Francis. And she has listened to your Arguments, you say, and seems Compliant?

Bellmine. Yes Sir, she has promis'd to comply with what I desired.

Enter Servant

[*Servant*]. Madam, here are some Ladies come to wait on you.   [*Exit*]

Lady Volant. Oh me! I wou'd not for a Kingdom be found alone Entertaining Men. This is a Censorious Town,   430 and I wou'd not give them an Advantage over my Bright Reputation.

Sir Francis. I believe it may be my Niece and Daughter, I order'd them to attend your Ladyship this Evening. Ay, 'tis so, 'tis so. Observe now, Sir, if she has not too much Wit, to be so Generous as to Marry you for Love only, and to trust to your Stars.

Enter Æmilia *and* Marina.

Freelove. I am sure if she Marrys for any other Reason, it shall not be me.

Lady Volant. I protest Ladies, were it any but you, who   440 surpriz'd me in this indecent Criminal Converse, I shou'd never have the assurance to obtrude my self upon Company again.

Æmilia. I assure your Ladyship, we have not perceived any thing Criminal; and if you please to keep your own Council, we are not at all Curious.

Lady *Volant.* Ay, but Madam, to be entertaining men alone, that's the thing grieves me.

Marina. (*Aside*) No, 'tis because that you have not a Man
450 alone, that's the thing Grieves you.

Lady *Volant.* For they are so Censorious here, that really I do not in all the Sphere of my Memory recollect one Woman whose Reputation is not Contaminated.

Marina. I am sorry to hear that.

Lady *Volant.* Your Ladyships excepted. Truth on't is, they make themselves obnoxious to such Calumnies by their Imprudent Behaviour. For was not my Lady *Courtly* seen twice in one week at the Play? and was not my Lady *Blameless* in a Mask in the Gallery? and was not Mrs. *Wellbred*
460 heard most Impiously and Obscenely to wish it were the Custom in this Town, for Women to sit in the Pit? and is not Mrs. *Winlove* seen to walk often in St. *Stephen's-Green.*

Marina. I beseech you, Madam, do not Censure Ladies for this, for I have been Guilty of all these things several times.

Lady *Volant.* What! and do you own it?

Æmilia. Certainly own it; for if there be a Fault in it, it is only when it is made a secret.

Lady *Volant.* Sir *Francis*, I protest you must pardon me, if I Conjecture these Ladies have strange Crude Notions of
470 Honour. [*Turning to them*] Well Ladies, you may do what you please, but I wou'd no more be Guilty of these things, than I wou'd sit at a Play in the second Row, which I think very improper for one of my Quality.

Bellmine. And Beauty, Madam.

Lady *Volant.* Oh Sir! why really I think it a Disgrace to both. But I hope you do not approve the Behaviour of some, who are remark'd for daily admitting the visits of Men.

Æmilia. I must Confess, Madam, I seldom refuse their visits whose Conversation I like.

Lady *Volant*. Oh hideous! what can you regard in Mens   480
Conversation, that is Divertive? they are all Insidious, you
may believe me. They are always pestring a Woman with
their Love, then they beg Liberty to repeat their Visits, and
implore a reciprocal Passion; and not contented with that,
they desire to wait on her abroad, nay, to meet 'em abroad
alone, and Mask'd, and when they have procur'd our Consent
so far, then they imprudently proceed to———

Marina. [*Quickly*] Good Madam, do not you proceed farther at this time.

Lady *Volant*. I was only going to Caution you of the   490
Danger, and warn you to keep them at a distance, a vast
distance, for some of 'em are so forward, that if we permit 'em
to squeeze our Hand, they will incontinently Write to us, and
the first Opportunity that offers, will force a Kiss, and they
have no sooner ravish'd that, but———

Æmilia. [*Interrupting*] Indeed, Madam, we want no Caution to avoid all this, nor shou'd I think any Man Impudent,
who attempted all these things, if I granted him any one of
them.

Lady *Volant*. 'Tis my great Concern for you, that's all; for   500
I wou'd have every ones Reputation as unsully'd as my own.

Freelove. (*Apart*) What a damn'd Malitious Jade it is!

Sir *Francis*. No Niece, you want no Caution in this matter;
but you do in another as Material as your Reputation; your
Fortune, I mean. For indeed who can preserve a Reputation
without Money, or if one shou'd, who regards it?

Freelove. So, now for a Lash at me.

Sir *Francis*. Look here, Niece, here is a Gentleman has given
himself the trouble to come hither to make Love to you, without having Money enough to pay for a License, or the   510
Wedding Dinner.

Freelove. Madam, I own.———

Sir *Francis* [*Interrupting*] Ay, ay, he owns it, what wou'd
you have more; a very honest undesigning Gentleman as ever
I saw.

Freelove. I have no hopes you shou'd ever have a favourable thought for me, if it is to be purchas'd with Wealth. But if the sincerest Passion, the humblest Adoration, a Heart im-mov'd by any thing but you, can atone for the want of
520 Wealth——

Sir *Francis.* Satisfy your self, Sir, they will not. Nor your fine Person, nor your Wit, nor your Courage, nor your Stars, nor a thousand things more. To convince you how small I think their Power, I will leave you in my Mistress's Lodgings. Come Girls, come away. Madam, as soon as I have dispos'd of my Daughter, I will beg to be made happy.

Æmilia. ⎱ Your Ladyships Servant.
Marina. ⎰

Lady *Volant.* Your most humble Servant. Nay, I will wait on you down. Do you think I wou'd be left alone with Men?

Exeunt omnes præter Freelove & Bellmine.

530 *Bellmine.* So you have very industriously ruin'd your self with the old Gentleman. But let us be gone before her Ladyship returns.

Freelove. Yes, he will avoid me as carefully as we wou'd an old cast Mistress.

Bellmine. But where is the necessity of perswading him you have no Estate?

Freelove. That *Æmilia* may be the more convinc'd it is so.

Bellmine. Wou'd you have her Love a Man because he is poor?

540 *Freelove.* No, but I wou'd not have her forbear it for that Reason.

Bellmine. He will make use of all his Power to oppose you.

Freelove. The better still; I shall make the stronger tryal of her Love.

When Love's sincere, no Enterprize is hard;
And Wealth and Titles then bear no Regard.

Exeunt.

ACT IV

Scene St. Stephen's-Green

Trickwell *and* Timothy *Meet.*

Trickwell. SURE I shou'd know that Face. My old
Acquaintance *Timothy* in Being!

Timothy. What, my dear Rakehell alive still!

Trickwell. Nor Time nor thy Disguise can hide thee from
me.

Timothy. I think indeed it is five years since we have seen
each other; but what Disguise prithee?

Trickwell. Why that bloated Belly, and those bladder Cheeks,
that Crimson Hue, and those huge Pillars which support thee.
Thou wer't as Wan and Thin when last I saw thee, as if you   10
were just escaped from the Gallies.

Timothy. Ease and Plenty have made this Alteration, Eating
well, and Lying soft. Thank my Stars, I thrive very well in
this Country.

Trickwell. Then I suppose you Despise it.

Timothy. That's but an odd Reason.

Trickwell. A very common one; for I have observ'd that
none Despise *Ireland* so much as those who thrive best in it.
And none are so severe in their Reflections upon it, as those
who owe their Birth and Fortune to it; I have known many of   20
'em, when they come first to *London*, think there is no way
so ready to purchase the Title of a Wit, as to Ridicule their
own Country.

But tell me, hast thou thrust thy self into any Business?
Hast thou got any Employment?

Timothy. Yes, a very pleasant one, I am in keeping.

Trickwell. In keeping!

Timothy. Ay, I am kept.

Trickwell. Kept!

30 *Timothy.* Kept! ay kept; so I say, don't you hear?

Trickwell. But not understand. Kept! for what in the name
of *Venus*? to roll on some Body's Bowling Green?

Timothy. Well, Sir, you may be as merry as you please with
my Shape, but I have other secret Charms, Sir, I have. For
know that I have been in keeping these three years, and by a
fine Lady; A Witty Lady.

Trickwell. And a Rich one?

Timothy. Not altogether so Rich, as when I knew her first,
but she has somewhat left still.

40 *Trickwell.* Then I suppose as her Fortune declines, so does
your Passion. And so you are now about quitting her.

Timothy. But like a Man of Honour, not till I have first
provided for her; I am about Marrying her to a considerable
Man.

Trickwell. O Rare *Tim*! now her Name?

Timothy. I know thou art a Trusty Dog, or I had not told
you so much; but in a little time you shall know all. And now
pray give me an account of your Affairs, for I think you seem
to be much in the same Circumstances as formerly.

50 *Trickwell.* I do but seem to be so. You must know I'm
Marry'd.

Timothy. See the difference of our Cases, how I thrive upon
one, more than you on the other. But pray let me know farther.

Trickwell. You remember about five years ago, I waited on
Collonel *Worthy*; I attended him to *Flanders*, where he was
kill'd, but before he dy'd, for some secret services, he gave
me all his Cloaths and Linning and Fifty Guineas.

Timothy. Lucky Rogue! sure you fancy'd your self a
Collonel then?

Trickwell. No, I had the humility to dispense with the   60
Title of Captain, which I assum'd immediately after my
Arrival in *London*; 'tis true I pretended to an Estate too, and
so went a Fortune hunting.

Timothy. Very prudently done.

Trickwell. In short, I met with a Lady who was on the
same scent; and we Believ'd, Cheated, and Marry'd each
other.

Timothy. The common Fate of Fortune-hunters. But what
is become of your Spouse?

Trickwell. I can no more give you a particular account of   70
her, than how I spent my fifty Guineas. She first apprehended
the Cheat, and taking the opportunity of my being Drunk one
Night, march'd off, and I never heard of her since. In a little
time after having lost my Wife, pawn'd my Cloaths, and spent
all my Money; I return'd to my old way of Living, and have
got into a good Service again.

Timothy. So 'tis but the Right about as you were.

Trickwell. I wish I cou'd find her out tho', not out of the
least Passion for her Person, but her Fortune, for she has
some. Here comes the Gentleman I now serve, an Admirable   80
Man.

Timothy. I saw him to day. But they say he is poor.

Enter Freelove *and* Bellmine.

Trickwell. You must know that——

Bellmine. Come hither, Good Sir.

Trickwell. [*To* Timothy] We'll talk another time.

Timothy. Well, well, Adieu.   *Exit.*

Bellmine. With your Master's Leave, I have an Affair,
which I can only trust a Man of your Diligence and Art with.

Trickwell. Your most humble Servant, Sir, I will discharge
it accordingly.   90

Bellmine. You see that Gentleman that comes this way.

Trickwell. Him with the Two Ladies?

Bellmine. The same. This is Sir *Francis Feignyouth*; go to

him directly, he does not know you, and with all the Cunning
you have perswade him there is a Lady desperately in Love
with him.

Trickwell. With an old Man, Sir!

Bellmine. Have a little patience. First fire him with a
description of her, and when you find him eager; seem to
100 have taken him for me all the while, that will vex him. Then
advise him to come disguis'd, and pass for me, and assure him
she shall meet him here this Evening, and let him know he
may be very free with her.

Trickwell. It shall be done, Sir.

Bellmine. Well, walk on a little, that you may not be seen
talking to us.   *Exit* Trickwell.

Freelove. And so you design he shall meet my Lady *Volant*
in your place. What will be the effect of that?

Bellmine. He will discover that she had an Appointment
110 with me, and if he is not stark mad, it will Convince him what
a Creature she is.

Freelove. But is this very Honourable in you to deceive a
poor Lady thus?

Bellmine. It wou'd be much less Honourable to suffer him
to Marry her; for he will not be perswaded but she is very
Rich.

Freelove. He mistakes her for a Woman of Wit too; But I
fancy except Virtue, that is the greatest want she has.

Bellmine. She has some Wit when she talks to Inferiour
120 People; but when in Conversation with those of Fashion and
of Sense, she endeavours to elevate her Thoughts, (as she calls
it) and refine her Language, and makes both unintelligible,
so is affectedly Ridiculous. To be Witty she spoils her Language, and her Language confounds even what is Wit.

Freelove. 'Tis strange he shou'd be blind to so many Faults;
but you are in the right to prevent his Ruin, since you hope
to Marry his Daughter. Do you start at the Word?

Bellmine. The nearer the Precipice, the more it dazles my
sight and understanding. Why you us'd to dislike the thing

as much as I, till you saw this *Æmilia*; and remember if e're   130
I am weary of the Bondage, 'twas by your Example I sub-
mitted to it. Tho' I expect to be thought the more prudent
Person, who have my fancy for the Lady back'd with a good
Fortune.

Freelove. You deserv'd to be ill us'd for your suspitions; and
may be no greater a Gainer than I am; for (as the World
goes) whatever Fortune the Lover gains by his Mistress, 'tis
ten to one but the Husband will repay with Interest, to get rid
of his Wife. I hope we shall succeed, and shall have no reason
to Repent. I am impatient to know my Fate; Let us lose no   140
time; your Emissary's Discourse with Sir *Francis* may give us
an Opportunity to speak to the Ladies; I see them coming, let
us walk on.   *Exeunt.*

Enter Sir Francis Feignyouth, Æmilia *and* Marina,
follow'd by Trickwell.

Trickwell. Sir, will you be pleas'd to favour me with a
Minuits Audience?

Sir *Francis.* What's thy Business?

Trickwell. I wou'd wish you were alone, Sir. I have something to deliver to you from a fair Lady.

Sir *Francis.* [*To the Women*] Em——walk on, I'll overtake
you, this is my Lawyers Servant about an Extraordinary   150
Affair. [*To* Trickwell] And what Commands pray has this
same fair Lady for me?   [*Exeunt the Women*]

Trickwell. Commands! alack, alack, poor Soul she has no
Commands, no Sir, her Empire's at an end, and conferr'd on
you. *Don Cupid* has taken stand on your shoulders, and with
all his might has shot her thro' and thro'.

Sir *Francis.* Heark ye Friend, if you wou'd have me believe
you are in earnest, speak sense, speak sense d'ye see, and don't
prate to me of Empires, and *Don Cupids*, and Darts, and such
stuff, but tell me plainly, and in short, what it is you wou'd   160
be at.

Trickwell. Well then, Sir, since you will have it without any

Decoration or Preamble, you shall; and truly Sir, I do not wonder you are impatient to know, that the prettiest Woman, the sweetest Woman, the wittiest Woman, and till she saw you, the modestest Woman even in her heart, shou'd slight all the Men in Town, and fall desperately in Love with you, only upon seeing you.

Sir *Francis.* Do not you banter now my Friend? hah! do
170   not you banter?

Trickwell. To Convince you I do not, Sir, I will tell you where you shall see her, and I will not take one Penny for my pains.

Sir *Francis.* Two of the best Proofs a Man wou'd desire. But to raise my Spirits a little, pray tell me what sort of a Woman is she?

Trickwell. Why Sir, in the first place then, she is of a considerable Family.

Sir *Francis.* Phoo, Pox of her Family.
180   *Trickwell.* And of a most accomplish'd Education——

Sir *Francis.* A Pox of her Education too; that may render all her other Beauties useless.

Trickwell. I mean, Sir, she Sings, Dances, Plays on several Instruments, speaks French, and the like, Sir.

Sir *Francis.* Ay, now thou say'st something. But her Person, let me hear somewhat of that. She is not little?

Trickwell. Of middle Stature.

Sir *Francis.* That's well; I hate a Dwarf and a Maypole. A little Frisking, Jumping, tumbling Ball; and a Long, Thin,
190   Scraggy, ungainly Lath. Her Complexion next.

Trickwell. Like her Stature, between Extreams; Neither White nor Brown; Sanguine, but no fix'd Red, except upon her Lips, a faint Blush seems always rising in her Face, but clearest on her Cheeks.

Sir *Francis.* Admirable, admirable! not Lean you say.

Trickwell. No Grape that's kindly Ripe, can be
            So Round, so Plump, so Soft as she.

You know the Song.

Sir *Francis.* I am all on Fire. Delicate Creature! I have done with my Lady *Volant*, that's certain. I do not want 200 Money, why then shou'd I be a Slave for it? Now her Eyes, her Eyes, if they prove right!

Trickwell. Of a sprightly Blew.

Sir *Francis.* That's not so well. I cou'd wish 'em Languishing, and of a Glossy Black.

Trickwell. See them, see them, Sir, and dislike 'em if you can. But her Temper is so Gentle, so Meek——

Sir *Francis.* Oh I abhor a Termagant; I hate a Mistress that a Man must go to Cuffs with. I wou'd have her just such a Woman as you Describe her, Soft, and Compliant; only her 210 Eyes, I cou'd wish her Eyes were Black.

Trickwell. Ne're mind the Colour, Sir, 'tis not the Colour makes the Eye beautiful, 'tis the shape of it, the Lustre.

Sir *Francis.* Well, well, go on with her Description.

Trickwell. Her Teeth are small, even, white and clean; smooth, and look as if just polish'd.

Sir *Francis.* If she answers this Description, I will make thy Fortune, thou hast made me already fancy my self Happy, I am in Raptures. [*He muses*] But go on, go on, be never silent in her praise. I am sorry her Eyes a'n't Black tho'. 220

Trickwell. 'Twere endless, to recount all her Perfections; but to conclude, Sir, to prove how large a share she has of Wit and Judgment, this delicate Creature, with thousand other Charms, all in their Bloom, offers her Heart to you.

Sir *Francis.* Patience, Patience! I am Five and twenty again, Eighteen, and shall I have the riffling of all these Charms say'st thou?

Trickwell. For my part, I believe she will deny you nothing. No one that Loves so much can. In sleep she dreams of you, and all her waking hours are spent in sighs and wishes for her 230 admir'd Charming *Bellmine.*

Sir *Francis.* The Devil! for whom?

Trickwell. For her dear Lovely *Bellmine.*

Sir *Francis.* For the Devil.

Trickwell. What mean you, Sir?

Sir *Francis.* For *Bellmine*! ah Plague is all this meant to him!

Trickwell. Meant to him! why are not you Mr. *Bellmine*? did she not point you to me this very day as you walk'd here
240   with three or four more?

Sir *Francis.* No Sir, I am not Mr. *Bellmine*, nor have I been like him these Twenty years. A Curse on your mistake! that has kindled all this Fuel within me for nothing. I am struck cold already, I fancy my self Fourscore. But Sirrah, I'll be reveng'd on you for giving me these hopes to no purpose. I wou'd not have been balk'd thus for a Thousand Pound.

Trickwell. I am sure Sir, if it be not you, that she Loves, I cou'd wish it were you. I have a greater Inclination for your Service than for his.

250   Sir *Francis.* What good, will your Inclinations or Wishes do me?

Trickwell. Why, a great deal Sir; since I have committed this mistake, I will persevere in it.

Sir *Francis.* How, how!

Trickwell. I have already betray'd the poor Lady's Secrets, and to make you amends for this Disturbance, I will order matters so, that you shall be the happy Man.

Sir *Francis.* I burn again. Let me Embrace thee. But the Way, the Way, the Method, my dear Rogue!

260   *Trickwell.* You shall meet her, and act like him.

Sir *Francis.* That will be somewhat difficult, I fear me, for an old Man.

Trickwell. For once, Sir, you may do well enough. I will perswade her to meet you here this Evening as soon as it is growing dark; she shall come in a Mask, and do you come muffled in a Cloak; she is so excessively Fond of Mr. *Bellmine*, that I am sure, she will comply with my Proposal, and with his Desires; therefore you may be very Free with her, hurry her immediately into a Coach; and Fear will make her yield
270   to love, as Love wou'd to him.

Sir *Francis*. Excellent, Excellent! I shall not contain my self till the happy hour. But will not you play the Rogue, and deceive me?

Trickwell. Upon my Honour, Sir, it shall be as I say.

Sir *Francis*. Enough. The Honour of a Pimp is sacred. The next thing dear to him is Gold; here are five Guineas for you before hand, that thy Honour may be more sacred; (and pray consider how Guineas are rais'd) and if I find every thing answerable to what you have said, I will Love her, and Reward thee immoderately. I will go and prepare my self, and be sure you be punctual.   *Exit.*   280

Trickwell. *How sweet the Profit, how deserv'd the Gain,*
            Which we as a Reward t'our Wit obtain.

Now to give an account of my Negotiation.

            Enter Freelove *and* Æmilia; Bellmine *and* Marina.

Bellmine. At least Madam, you must acknowledge I am industrious for the good of your Family.

Marina. And I suppose, I must be Claim'd as a Reward for your good Service to my Father.

Æmilia. For my part, I doubt the success of your Design; for I have so good an Opinion of my Uncle, that I do not think he will be perswaded to meet a Mask. I am sure he rails against such People more than any Man.   290

Freelove. Railing is no more a sign of Virtue, than of Wit. In this age People are seldom what they seem; there are some go to Church without Devotion. We have Criticks without Wit or Judgment; and some Fight without Courage; and there are Women very precise without Virtue. And I equally suspect the Woman who Boasts her Virtue, and the Man who Boasts his Valour; and it generally has the same effect, we are picked at it, and provok'd to destroy their Reputation.   300

Bellmine. To Convince you, Madam, we make a right Judgment of Sir *Francis*; Come hither *Trickwell*, and give an Account how you have succeeded.

Trickwell. I have succeeded as much to your Desires, Sir, as

for my own Profit. Witness this Gold, Sir. Thus has he
Rewarded me for Obeying you.

Bellmine. What do you think now, Madam? You behav'd
your self very Cunningly to get Money from him. Yet I have
often known Men Starve their Family, and Feast their
310   Mistress.

Trickwell. I remember, Sir, I heard you give a Description
of one of your Mistresses, and I entertain'd him with that,
which agreed almost perfectly with what he Admires. He is
gone in Raptures, to prepare himself for the wish'd for hour.

Marina. And you depend on my Lady *Volant's* coming?

Bellmine. I have Enticed her by the hopes both of Love and
Profit; which will make her as punctual to me, as a Sharper
wou'd be to a young Rich Cully he had Set. She will no more
fail meeting me, than Mrs. *Flippant,* with her new Equipage,
320   wou'd miss the *Strand* on a *Sunday.*

Æmilia. If she be such a Woman, 'twill be Charity to
prevent the Match. But I fancy, Mr. *Bellmine,* you have
some self Interest in this Matter : You expect my Cousin's
Fortune shou'd be encreas'd by this, to make you digest
Matrimony the better, for I hear you have dreadful apprehensions of it, and are resolv'd to have a great Fortune.

Bellmine. Both Reports of me have been truth, I must
confess, Madam; but the more I see this Lady, the more my
Aversion for the one, and my Regard for the other, are
330   lessen'd.

Æmilia. If you Marry for Money, you must expect to be
severely Censured by one who has none.

Freelove. But Madam, you will not have favourable Thoughts
for one who knows that, and yet dies for you. Who wou'd
sacrifice his Life to be in that state which he there dreads.

Æmilia. But have you Consider'd all the Inconveniencies
of Marrying a Woman without a Fortune?

Freelove. All, all Madam; and wou'd undergo a thousand
more for you.

340   *Æmilia.* And how you will be laugh'd at by the World.

Freelove. I'll pitty their Ignorance. I have Consider'd all Madam, all the Hazards, all the Inconveniencies; how difficult to have a Man's Behaviour approv'd by all, that it is impossible to be thought a Kind Husband by the Women, and a prudent one by the Men. But you shall ever Rule your Conduct and my Heart. I give my Heart without Reserve, had I the World, I wou'd bestow it so. I will be still your Slave, still gaze upon those Eyes, and every look shall make me more your Slave. Oh I want words to tell how truly I adore you! or had I words that were Expressive, my Passion is too fierce   350
to utter them.

Æmilia. If you declare your real Thoughts, your Passion cannot be greater than your Generosity; and may be easier Feign'd. You see I listen to your Love, because I believe it disinterested; if I thought it were not, not all your Art shou'd gain a Moments Audience. I hear you talk of Love; tho' I were silent, to hear, gives hopes.

Freelove. Let me for ever talk, and only talk of Love. To Love be all the Business of my Life; it were abuse of Life to Live to any other End, be every Moment so employ'd; I talk,   360
but it is Faint and Mean; my Heart now swells, and seems to heave and rage, that I no better can describe its Passion. It bids me say, amongst a thousand things that crowd upon my Tongue, I cannot Love you more, I ne're will Love you less.

Bellmine. (*Aside*) It wou'd be a damn'd unconscionable thing now in her, to remember all this after Marriage; for 'tis as unreasonable for Women to expect Love after enjoyment, as for a Man who had spent his Fortune, to expect as much Credit as when he had it in possession.   370

Marina. What is that you mutter of unconscionable?

Bellmine. Why, I say it is an unconscionable thing of you both, to keep us in pain thus, when you may so easily remove it. And to seem to doubt our Passion, when we offer so fair to prove it.

Marina. And what is that, Good Sir?

Bellmine. What I cou'd never bear the sound of, till those bewitching Eyes of yours sweeten'd it: Marriage.

380 *Marina.* Why do you expect that I shou'd disobey my Father?

Bellmine. Why do you suppose that I expect you will be obedient to him?

Æmilia. Nay Cousin, you need not fear he will oppose you; but I owe some Obedience to an Uncle too, and I am very sure, I never shall have his Consent. But we'll talk no farther of this Matter, till we see what becomes of his Intrigue.

Marina. I think the Hour of the Lovers Meeting is almost come. I suppose you will hover hereabout, to see what will be the Issue of it.

390 *Bellmine.* It may be some diversion to you Ladies to be Witness to it.

Æmilia. No, that will not be so proper; we shall be satisfied to receive an account of it from you. Till when your Servant.

Freelove. Tho' griev'd to part, I ought not to Complain, since you have bid me hope.

                    Exeunt Freelove, Bellmine *and* Trickwell.

Marina. Prithee *Æmilia*, why wou'd you put this Constraint upon your Inclinations? I am sure you had rather he had stay'd, I read it in your looks; I found your Eyes had almost betray'd your Heart.

400 *Æmilia.* I found so too. That made me more desirous he shou'd be gone. I have Confest enough for this time.

Marina. Yes truly, so you have, since you design to Marry him. For Men's Importunity and our Shyness have the same end.

> *Their subtle Sex is violent to Gain,*
> *And we Deny, more surely to Obtain.*

                                        Exeunt.

ACT V.

Scene Continues.

Enter Sir Francis Feignyouth *in a Cloak.*

Sir *Francis.* **Y**ONDER she comes; now if I can Disguise my self till I get her to a Coach, she's my own. Wou'd it were a little darker however.

Enter Lady Volant *Mask'd.*

Lady *Volant.* Who is there? Mr. *Bellmine.*

Sir *Francis.* The same.

Lady *Volant.* You see, Dear Sir, what an excessive Sovereignty you have over me, to compel me to meet you. But you have an irresistible way with you; and all the World extols you for a Man of Honour, and I hope you will behave your self like one to me.   10

Sir *Francis.* (*Apart*) Methinks I shou'd know that Voice.

[*To her*] I, I, my Dear, I will; I'll make your Fortune.

Lady *Volant.* Your obedient Servant, Dear Sir; indeed it is as uncommon to meet with a Generous Lover in this profligate Age, as with a Secret or a Constant one. But I Conjecture you to have all these Virtues, or I had not consented to meet you at first Request.

Sir *Francis.* (*Apart*) First Request! What a Pox does she mean? I'm certain I know her voice.

Lady *Volant.* (*Aside*) Pray Heaven, I be not mistaken in   20
my Man. [*To him*] But now I have met you, sure you can desire no more.

Sir *Francis*. (*Aside*) By all that's Virtuous, my Lady *Volant*!
Is she the amorous Lady? This was a lucky Discovery; I'll try
her farther. [*To her*] Come my dear, I am impatient till we
are more private, I have a Coach waiting at the end of the
Green.

Lady *Volant*. I'll wait on you immediately. (*Aside*) Oh
Heavens! how near was I to be ruin'd! This is Sir *Francis*!
30 what can this mean? ha! I have it now. A Trick of that
Villain *Bellmine*'s to prevent our Marriage; but I'll be even
with him.

Sir *Francis*. Come, are you ready?

Lady *Volant*. Ungrateful Worthless Fellow! (*Unmasking*)
Not only base thy self, but wou'd have me too, share thy
Guilt: how canst thou be that Mercenary Wretch, to Abuse
thy Noble Friend Sir *Francis Feignyouth*, to deceive his
Virtuous Beautiful Daughter, forsake and leave her when the
Match is concluded on, and Marry me, because I am Weal-
40 thier? But tho' thou woud'st be so Base, think you I am so?
Do you imagine I wou'd be unjust to him, a Man of that
Worth, that Honour, so fine a Gentleman, because you
proffer'd me a larger Settlement? No, coud'st thou give me
this Island, I wou'd refuse it, and rather starve with him.

Sir *Francis*. Now, let me never drink Claret more, if I can
tell what it is you mean by all this.

Lady *Volant*. Who do I see? Sir *Francis*! It seems then you
came with a Design to meet some Lewd Woman; oh me
unfortunate! is there nothing but Treachery and Inconstancy
50 in the Sex? Have I refus'd so many great Matches, and at
last Consented to be yours, and is this my Reward?

Sir *Francis*. Why, as I take it, my Good Lady, you came
with a Design to meet some Body too.

Lady *Volant*. If my Trouble wou'd give me leave to speak!
That Traytor *Bellmine*, whom you intrusted to plead for you,
offer'd to forsake your Daughter, and Marry me himself——

Sir *Francis*. And so you met him to that purpose.

Lady *Volant*. Han't I already told you how I resented his

Baseness, when I thought you were he. 'Tis true I consented
to meet him, in hopes to perswade him to a more Virtuous   60
and Just Proceeding. I wou'd have conceal'd his Crime from
you, being always inclin'd to do Good!

Sir *Francis.* Oh the damn'd young Rogue, I'll be so Reveng'd on him——

Lady *Volant.* [*Quickly*] And thus while I endeavour'd to do
your Family Service, even at the hazard of my Reputation;
you suspect me. This is a plain Conspiracy between you both
to ruin me; is this like a Man of Honour? this the Behaviour
I hop'd for from the worthy Sir *Francis*! I am ruin'd, undone,
betray'd; what will become of me?   70

Sir *Francis.* Nay hear me, Good Lady, do but hear me.

Lady *Volant.* No, I will never hearken to Man more. I will
retire from the World, and leave my Wealth to erect Hospitals
to maintain Mad men and Fools; rather than enrich the
unjust.

Sir *Francis.* Hear me but speak.

Lady *Volant.* That Sir *Francis Feignyouth* shou'd suspect
me! the only Person in the World I ever gave the least
Encouragement to; I easily cou'd revenge my self, by marrying *Bellmine*, and deprive you both of my Fortune, and of   80
your Son-in-Law; had I not still a zeal for your interests, and
an Abhorrence for his Treachery.

Sir *Francis.* Come, I'll tell you how we shall be both reveng'd
on this Insinuating, Wheedling, Deceitful young Dog. I'll
Marry you instantly, and will not give him the value of a
Rapparee Farthing with my Daughter.

Lady *Volant.* Why verily Sir *Francis*, you speak like a Man
of Honour; indeed to Marry an injur'd Woman, is the only
way to do her Right. But I can hardly Reinstate you in my
good Opinion, sufficiently to Consent to that yet.   90

Sir *Francis.* Nay, I will not delay it a moment; I have a
Chaplain ready at my House, and we will spend the Night
in Embraces, and Laughing at this Impudent Cozening
Knave.——See where he comes, if I were not about taking a

surer and sweeter Revenge, I wou'd cut his Throat directly.
Lady *Volant*. For Virtues sake, let us be gone, I have that
Detestation for a Cheat, that I cannot brook his appearance.

Enter Bellmine *and* Freelove.

Bellmine. We may venture to approach them now; we shall
confound her more, tho' I suppose he is already sufficiently
100 convinc'd what a Virtuous Lady she is.
Sir *Francis*. (*To* Freelove *Entring*.) Your Servant, your
Servant, Sir, my Honest, Faithful, Plotting, Undermining,
Dear, Half-witted Rival and Son-in-Law! This was a rare
Design of yours, an admirable Design.
Bellmine. Sir!
Sir *Francis*. A curious Design, a deep Design! Oh these
young Fellows are subtle Dogs at a Plot!
Bellmine. What wou'd you be at, Sir?
Sir *Francis*. What wou'd you be at, Sir, this Lady, Sir. But
110 I shall prevent you, Sir, for I am going to be Marry'd to her
instantly, Sir.
Bellmine. You are not serious sure? why Sir, I'll convince
you that——
Lady *Volant*. [*Quickly*] Oh I cannot bear that Traytors
sight, let us be gone, I shall faint, if I stay a moment longer.
He will have the impudence to deny he made Love to me,
and desir'd a Meeting.
Bellmine. I own I did, Sir, but——
Sir *Francis*. Oh! Did you so? truth will out.
120 *Bellmine*. And I design'd——
Sir *Francis*. To Marry her your self——Not a word more,
Sir, nor a step farther——In half an hours time, I'll admit
you to wish me Joy. And so your Servant.
Lady *Volant*. Your Servant Good Mr. Little-plot. Ha, ha.
Exeunt Sir Francis *and Lady* Volant.
Bellmine. What is the meaning of all this? I cannot under-
stand it.
Freelove. To me the matter is very plain. She has out-witted

you; and made him believe you wou'd have Marry'd her;
this you see has enrag'd him against you; and being Mad
enough to think her Rich, and to be Reveng'd on you, he is 130
gone to Marry her.

Bellmine. He will be Ruin'd, Undone, Beggard.

Freelove. And *Marina* the less Fortune. That Consideration
is of no small moment to you.

Bellmine. Your Example is of so much greater weight with
me, that it has not only reconcil'd me to Marriage, but I
think in my Conscience, I cou'd Marry *Marina* without a
Fortune. But it mads me that she shou'd have such a Mother-
in-Law.

Freelove. She will not be much improv'd by her Example. 140

Bellmine. As much as a Man may improve himself in Conversation, by Drinking with the silent Club here.

Freelove. 'Tis such an improvement as Expert Musitians
receive by hearing Bunglers, she may learn what to avoid.

Bellmine. But is there no way to prevent it?

Freelove. None, that I know of, unless you had some fresh
Matter to urge against her. And here comes the likeliest Man
to assist you, to furnish you with Scandal.

Bellmine. This will be Joyful News to him. Oh he is so
facetious when any one has been Guilty of an indiscretion, 150
and has so many smart Jokes upon the Unfortunate!

Enter Wormwood.

Wormwood. Your Servant Gentlemen. My Spleen has been
so tickled just now, at the most diverting sight. Ha, ha.

Bellmine. What, has any one broke his Neck? or has some
young Lady run away with her Brothers Footman? or is the
hopeful Son expell'd the Colledge? or has there been a Fire
lately in Town? or any Merchants broke?

Wormwood. Almost as Comical as any of these. I just now
met Sir *Francis Feignyouth* handing my Lady *Volant* into his
House, he told me he was that Moment going to be Marry'd, 160
and bid me come to you to be Confirm'd of the Truth.

Ha, ha.

Bellmine. And is this so great a Jest?

Wormwood. Ay, is it not? to have an old Fellow, who is so fond of Whoring and Freedom and Money, make himself a Slave to Marry a Beggar; that she is one I am now convinc'd. Come, will you along with me, I have a Cordial for him that will spoil the effects of Sack-Posset. I suppose the Business is finish'd by this time, he shall not know it before. 170 'Tis such a Jest!

Bellmine. No, no, I am Melancholly enough already, and thy Jests always give me the Spleen.

Wormwood. Well, I'll go alone then, for I long to plague him.   *Exit.*

Freelove. That a Fellows whole Delight shou'd be the Torment of others.

Enter Trickwell.

Trickwell. Sir, Sir, I have rare News for you. I have found out that will break off Sir *Francis*'s Match.

Bellmine. Be quick in telling it.

180 *Trickwell.* Hearing you in great concern to day for his Design to Marry my Lady *Volant*, I went immediately to her pretended Steward, who you must know, Sir, is my old Acquaintance.

Bellmine. The properest Person to detect her.

Trickwell. And wheedled him into a Confession that she has kept him two or three years.

Bellmine. Kept him! To what End?

Trickwell. Why, faith Sir, I believe to much the same End, that you kept the Fine Lady that Lodg'd in *Convent-Garden*.

190 *Bellmine.* This indeed may do, if the Intelligence comes not too late; but can you produce him that we may Confront her with him.

Trickwell. He is waiting for me at the end of the Walk.

Bellmine. Hast to him then, and pretend his Lady wants him; send him to us at Sir *Francis Feignyouth*'s, and wait you below till I call.

Trickwell. It shall be done, Sir.

Bellmine. Excellent Fellow! For thy Reward, if thy hopeful Spouse be in this Country, I'll find her out for you; But away.   *Exit* Trickwell.   200

Come *Freelove*, you will go with me, you may have an opportunity to see your *Æmilia.*

Freelove. That Consideration will carry me any where.

                                            Exeunt.

[Scene ii]

The Scene Changes

to Sir Francis Feignyouth's *House.*

Enter Sir Francis Feignyouth *and Lady* Volant.

Sir *Francis.* COME, Lady, now you are mine in spite of all my Rivals. I'll have them all to Supper, to Triumph over them. We will have nothing but Revelling, Feasting and Kissing, for our first Month at least. But we'll go to Bed soon, because the Drums and Trumpets will Disturb us early.

Lady *Volant.* (*Aside*) You will find some Duns in the Morning will disturb your Rest much more than they.

Sir *Francis.* What says Your Ladyship?

Lady *Volant.* Only contemplating on my Good Fortune.   10

Sir *Francis.* I'll give you no leisure to contemplate; you shall be busied with Action. I have sent to invite my Rivals from *Bellmine* down to *Vainly*; I'd not give a Farthing for a Jewel I must always keep lockt up in my Cabinet. I Love to publish my Happiness. But where are these Girls run?——This Marriage has set them a Madding now to be at it too—— Here Niece, Daughter, where are you?

Enter Æmilia *and* Marina.

I am sorry, Niece, your Admirer has no Estate, that you
might not lye alone to Night.

20   *Æmilia.* If I like his other Qualifications well enough to
Marry him, that shall be no Objection.

Sir *Francis.* (*Aside*) She is stark Mad; I must Marry my
Daughter as soon as I can, or she may Debauch her to the
same Design. [*Aloud*] But I am resolv'd nothing shall Dis-
compose me to Night. I have sent for some Musick to
Entertain you; Desire them to walk in, and show their Art.

[*Enter* Musicians.]

A Dialogue.

Set by Mr. *LEVERIDGE*.

He,   **Y**OU Bellamira *we Admire,*
         Which pleases you, tho' ill you use us;
      You wou'd taste Joys, which we desire,
30   *And Punish both, when you refuse us.*

She,   *Those Joys I'd keep as well as taste,*
         But both by yielding are destroy'd;
      For Men are ever in such haste,
         E're we have tasted, they are cloy'd.

He,   *All Humane Things their Crisis have,*
         To which arriv'd, they fade away;
      So long for Love you make us crave,
         E're you Consent, our flames decay.

She,   *On what strange Diet Lovers Live!*
     On hopes the Fair may be enjoy'd;   40
     Love even can Despair survive,
     But is by nourishment destroy'd.

He,   *Insatiate! I'd my Love repeat,*
     Only to breathing time agree;
     Because I cannot always Eat,
     Will you both Starve your self and me.

She,   *I grieve* Philander *to deny,*
     And yet I loose you if I grant;
     Not I alone can Satisfy,
     Without Variety you want.   50

He,   *Each Part Variety affords,*
     Your Hand, your Eyes, your Lips, your Breast;
     Believe this Kiss, if not my Words,
     For Love by Action's best exprest.

Chorus.

He,   *Believe this Kiss, if not my Words,*
     For Love by Action's best exprest.
She, *That I'll believe, tho' not your Words,*
     For Love by Action's best exprest.

[*Applause. Exeunt* Musicians.]

Enter Vainly *and* Wormwood.

Vainly. Why, it is impossible, Mr. *Wormwood,* that she
cou'd be false to me; I will not believe she is Married.   60
Wormwood. No, if thou wert Marry'd to her, you wou'd
not believe your self a Cuckold, tho' you saw her a Bed with
another Man.
Sir *Francis.* You are welcome, Gentlemen. Mr. *Vainly,* our
Quarrels are at an end now.
Wormwood. Then you are Marry'd. Ha, ha, ha——

Sir Francis. Why, that is kind to rejoyce at your Friends good Fortune.

Vainly. But, Madam, is it your way to receive Presents from one Man, and Marry another?

Sir Francis. How Presents!

Lady Volant. If one shou'd give attention to what every Fop says——

Wormwood. Nay, Sir *Francis*, be not angry at that. 'Twere happy for you, if she had receiv'd Presents enough to pay her Debts.

Sir Francis. What is't you mean, Sir?

Wormwood. That you have Marry'd one for Money, who owes more than she is Worth; That you will have a greater Crowd of Creditors at your Leve to Morrow Morning, than a New Favorite has of Flatterers. And for you, my Lady *Volant*, I heard Alderman *Formall* say to day, if you did not send the Three hundred Pounds you owe him, he wou'd sell your Plate to Morrow.

Sir Francis. I am confounded. What have you to answer to this?

Lady Volant. That if you think the Plate worth Redeeming, you had best send the Money.

Sir Francis. Impudence! I'll forswear my Marriage.

Lady Volant. I can easily prove it, if you do.

Sir Francis. Why are not you rich then?

Lady Volant. If I am not, you have enough to satisfie us both.

Sir Francis. I shall run Mad; I shall Burst. But come, answer me calmly.

Æmilia. So, now his Eyes begin to open.

Wormwood. I shall lose half my Pleasure, for want of some Body to help me to Torment him.

Vainly. If this be true; I believe she wou'd not Marry me, because she Lov'd me.

Enter Bellmine, Freelove *and* Timothy.

Bellmine. (*To* Timothy) Nay, no going back, or I'll spoil your going for ever. Sir *Francis*, your Servant. I hope I come time enough to prevent your Ruin.

Sir *Francis.* To Confirm it rather. Why they tell me that this Lady here is a Beggar.

Bellmine. I have brought one to Witness it. Sirrah, speak the Truth, if you expect to Live a moment.

Sir *Francis.* Oh are you there! That's well. Heark ye Slave have you not often swore to me, that my Lady *Volant* here was worth—— 110

Timothy. Not one shilling, Sir, that I know of.

Sir *Francis.* And am I Cheated, Chous'd, Fool'd, Abus'd, Ruin'd, Confounded, hah?

Timothy. Somewhat like it, truly Sir.

Sir *Francis.* I'll have her burnt for a Witch, and I'll have you flea'd you Dog. I'll do't my self.

Vainly. Ay, 'tis plain her tenderness of me, wou'd not let her Ruin me.

Bellmine. Hold, hold Sir, you have not yet heard the worst.

Sir *Francis.* Can any thing be worse? what! Can any thing be worse than Poverty? 120

Bellmine. You shall hear. Come Sirrah, make me a full Confession of all the Familiarities that have pass'd between you two.

Timothy. Alas Sir, wou'd you have me so ungenerous to Betray a Lady's Secrets?

Wormwood. Why this is Admirable, this is better sport than I expected.

Bellmine. No delay, or I'll saw your Windpipe this moment; Be quick, and let me not wast Breath on thee. 130

Sir *Francis.* And before mine is gone.

Timothy. Why then, Sir, if I must tell——But really 'tis not like a Man of Honour in Me.

Lady *Volant.* 'Tis no matter, *Timothy*; your Confession comes too late now to save him: 'Twill signify no more than a Pardon after Execution. (*Aside*) The more he knows the more he will give to be freed from me, and then I'll leave this hideous Country for ever.

Bellmine. What, are you already Marry'd? Have you made
140 such hast to be undone?

Sir *Francis.* Ay, ay, the Knot is ty'd; But come, go on, go on with your Confession.

Timothy. Then Sir, since I may speak, I have for about these three years liv'd with my Honour'd Lady there, as her Steward in Publick, and as her Husband in Private.

Sir *Francis.* Oh I faint! I dye, I dye! I'm a dead Man, I'm stone dead!   (*Sits down*)

Timothy. I think I had best sneak off before he comes to himself, least I shou'd be made to verify the Proverb, Confess
150 and be Hang'd.   *Exit.*

Marina. Good Sir, be pacify'd.

Sir *Francis.* Be pacify'd! Be damn'd; I'm in a fairer way for that. But I'll do one Meritorious Act first, I'll pluck her Heart out——Let me at her.   [*He runs at her*]

Lady *Volant.* At your Peril touch me; here are Witnesses enough, shou'd you offer me any Violence.

Vainly. Yes, yes Madam, I am bound in Conscience to be a Witness for you, because you Lov'd me too well to Marry me.

160 *Wormwood.* Fear him not, Madam; we will stand by you: Faith I Love thee better than ever, for the mischief thou hast done.

Sir *Francis.* Dost thou so, Tormentor? I'll have you two swing'd before I dye, that you may be Laugh'd at too. [*Calls*] Here, where are my Servants?

Wormwood. Come *Vainly*, we'll spare him the Trouble; let us to the Coffee-House, I burst till I publish this.

Vainly. Ay, pray let us go. Give ye Joy, Sir, Give ye Joy.
                              Exeunt Vainly *and* Wormwood.

Sir *Francis.* What had I to do with a Wife, what had I to
170 do with a Wife! Had I not Ease enough, had I not Freedom enough, had I not Wealth enough! I had every thing but

Wit enough.——Oh! I am a Jest to the World, a Scandal
to my Name, a Curse to my Family, and a Hell to my self.
Bellmine. You afflict your self too much.
Sir *Francis.* Impossible! Had she Virtue, that were some
atonement for her Poverty. Or had she been a Miss to some
Favorite, and beg'd an Estate of Forfeited Lands, that had
been some Comfort. But to be a Strumpet, and a poor
Strumpet!——
Bellmine. 'Tis but giving her separate Maintainance at   180
worst.
Sir *Francis.* No, no, I am resolv'd on it, I'll separate my self
from the World. [*Dramatically*] I am just going, just expiring,
Mr. *Bellmine,* I am wondrous faint on the suddain; all in a
cold sweat. But before I dye, let me dispose of my Family;
here Mr. *Bellmine,* take my Daughter, and all I have; you
deserve it for the Good you design'd me. But be sure to Plague
that Viper with Law, before she gets any thing.
Lady *Volant.* I despise your Malice, I'll have a share of
your Fortune spite of you all.   190
Bellmine. I hope, Madam, you will not oppose Sir *Francis's*
Design to make me the happiest of Men.
Marina. Since my Father has dispos'd of me, I own it is
according to my Inclinations.

Enter Trickwell *hastily to* Bellmine.

Trickwell. Sir, Sir, have you no more to do with *Timothy,*
I saw him steal away.
Bellmine. Nothing more. He has Confest all he told you
concerning that Lady.
Trickwell. Hah! What do I see?
Lady *Volant. Trickwell* there! Oh I am lost for ever.   200
                                        (*seems to faint*)
Sir *Francis.* A Judgment, a Judgment from Heaven! (*Start-
ing up.*) She dyes and I live.
Trickwell. Let her alone, I'll bring her to herself again.
Sir *Francis.* What, are you another of her Lovers?

Trickwell. No, no, Sir, I am none of her Lovers, for I am her Husband.

Omnes. How her Husband!

Lady *Volant.* Unlucky Wretch! What Devil sent thee here to my Undoing?

210   Sir *Francis.* I think thou wert the Spark that banter'd me this Evening so smartly. But no more fooling; I am in no Jesting humour.

Trickwell. Really Sir, I am so well acquainted with her Ladyship, that it is an Honour I shou'd not assume to my self, if it were not Truth.

Lady *Volant.* Fool, Thoughtless Sot! It were for thy Interest, as well as mine, to conceal this now; till I had got a Sum of Money to quit him. For know prating Brute, I have just Marry'd him.

220   *Trickwell.* Oh Wonderful!

Sir *Francis.* Oh wonderful Deliverance! Oh Blessing unthought of! I find my strength return; I shall live for ever. I am light as Air. I am in as much danger now of running Mad for Joy, as before for Grief. But take her to thee, go take her, and much good may she do ye.

Trickwell. Oh by no means Sir, after you is good manners, Sir, she is at your Service with all my heart and soul. Indeed Sir, she is.

Lady *Volant.* Be dumb for ever. Or talk his equal now, 230   thou canst do me no farther Mischief, nor can I longer bear thy sight. Farewel, and may each of you find his Wife, what you have taken such pains to prove me.   *Exit.*

Trickwell. Truly, I needed not have taken such pains to have known *Timothy*'s secrets.

Freelove. We need not wonder at her Rage. But *Trickwell*, is this the very Lady you Marry'd in *London* for a Fortune?

Trickwell. The very Numerical she, Sir; only she has chang'd her Name.

Sir *Francis.* Thou hast made such a happy Change in my 240   Fortune, that I will make thine; I will reward thee most profusely for this.

Freelove. (*To* Æmilia) Shall I be the only Man, who shall complain of Fortune? Shall Love so pure as mine meet no Reward?

Æmilia. Disinterested, Faithful Love, deserves a higher Reward than I can give.

Freelove. You are Reward above Man's Merit. Heaven can give no greater upon Earth.

Æmilia. And will you Marry a Woman that has nothing?

Freelove. Do not torture me with such Questions. I wou'd,   250
I wou'd, 'tis all I ask of Heaven.

Æmilia. Remember I have told you all the Inconveniencies.

Freelove. None, none, there can be none. 'Twere Luxury to starve with you. Pleasure and Freedom in a Goal.

Æmilia. Then take this earnest of a Heart, (*Giving her Hand*) as full of Generosity, as full of Love as yours.

Freelove. You give me endless, endless Joys.

Sir Francis. How, how, Niece, will you throw your self away thus? Marry a Man without a Fortune!

Æmilia. Even so, Sir. Nor shall I think my self thrown away   260
on him. Remember how lately you had been almost Ruin'd by Marrying for one.

Sir Francis. Well, do what you please, I shall never be angry again. A pretty Present this, Sir, she has made you. A fine Woman, and to my knowledge Twenty thousand Pounds ready Money.

Freelove. Had you the *Indies*, I cou'd not Love you more, but this is very surprizing.

Æmilia. It was an Uncle's Gift I had in *England*; and I   270
have industriously thus long conceal'd it, that I might not be pester'd by Fortune-hunters, and might be assur'd that he who Marry'd me, had no other Motive but Love. And I am happy that he prov'd so Generous, I Lik'd so well.

Bellmine. Nay then, Madam, I think I may Discover his secret now. Fate design'd you for each other. He too has had the same Design, you are not more alike in Tempers than in

Fortune. For I can assure you this Gentleman, who has given himself the Repute of being worth Nothing, has an Estate in *England* of Three thousand Pounds a Year.

280   Sir *Francis.* Admirable! Excellent! Nay, I always thought he deserv'd one. A most compleat Gentleman!

Freelove. [*To audience*]

   Let Misers be Enslav'd, and Drudge for Gain,
   Their Joys are False, tho' they their Wish Obtain.
   While no base Int'rest, Gen'rous Souls regard,
   And Love and Peaceful Minds be their Reward.

                        Exeunt Omnes.

FINIS.

EPILOGUE.

Spoke by Lady *Volant.*

WHO to a Monarch humbly sues for Grace,
  Shou'd not Consult the Merits of his Case,
So much, as those who offer his Address;
'Tis by their Int'rest he must hope Success.
Our Author thus, who can no Merit Plead,   ⎫
But the harsh Censures he deserve does dread,   ⎬
Orders that I for Mercy Intercede.   ⎭
He Judges right, but in his Choice he's out,
As he his Merit, I my Int'rest doubt.
And well I may; since 'tis by different Arts,   10
I must please Men, and gain the Ladies Hearts.
The Beaus I wou'd Oblige, but that you know
Is more than one poor Woman has Pow'r to do.
Besides they're all so Mercenary grown,
They'll grant no Favour, unless I grant one.
Their Answer is, when we a Boon demand,
Meet me at Chappellizard, or the Strand.
And that's a Bribe I think too dear to give,
To let this Play their dreadful Rage survive.
And from the Fair, what Mercy can be had!   20
I fear they'll hate me for but seeming Bad.
In hopes to please, now we have done the Play,
I'll throw the Nausceous Mask of Vice away.
And strive those Paths of Virtue to pursue,
So strictly kept, so eminent in you.

NOTES

Title page: *School-House-Lane*. "A narrow passage leading from the High-street to Cook-street was known at the commencement of the fifteenth century as 'le Ram Lane', apparently so styled from a building in High-street called 'Le Ramme'. The free school of the city of Dublin was subsequently erected in this locality, which thence acquired the name of the 'School-house lane'." John T. Gilbert, *History of the City of Dublin*, I, 237.

The printing house may have occupied the upper storey of a large house. In the *Dublin Scuffle* (1699), the London bookseller John Dunton refers to the premises of Brocas, Brent, and Powel as "Airy, Great and Noble . . . the *Top Printing-House* in all *Dublin*".

Title page: *John Brocas*. A reputable Dublin printer. John Dunton, who visited Dublin in 1698 for the purpose of selling books, paid tribute to Brocas as one of the three partners in the firm that published his catalogues. He paid special tribute to Brocas: "Mr *Brocas* is much of a Gentleman, he gave me a Noble Welcome to *Dublin*, and never grew less Obliging. He's one that loves his Friend as his Life . . . and I may say, without offence to the *Printers of Dublin*, that no Man in the Universe, better understands the *Noble Art and Mystery of Printing*, than John Brocas in *Skinner Row*." Dunton, *The Dublin Scuffle* (London, 1699), p. 139.

Epistle Dedicatory: *Earl of Inchiquin*. William O'Brien, Third Earl of Inchiquin, was born c. 1666 and had a full military and civil career. He was a member of the Irish House of Parliament from 1695, and in December 1697 he signed the declaration and association in defence of King William after an attempt on the king's life. He died in Co. Cork in 1719. (*Complete Peerage*.) It is interesting to note that Philips dedicated *Hibernia Freed* to a member of the other branch of the O'Brien family, i.e., Henry, Eighth Earl of Thomond (1688–1741). The latter became governor of Clare following the death of William, his cousin.

Epistle Dedicatory: Line 7. "Since the Humour the present Age is." The permissive spirit of the Restoration era was yielding to a more moral temper in the late sixteen nineties. See Introduction, pp. 33, 43.

Epistle Dedicatory: Line 36. "Wit." Perhaps the single most characteristic feature of Restoration comedy. It may be taken to mean 'invention', usually verbal (in the form of either epigrammatic observations or repartee), but also intellectual, in the sense of 'imagination' or *ingenium*, as Philips means it here. Cf. Thomas K. Fujimura, *The Restoration Comedy of Wit* (Princeton: University Press, 1952).

Epistle Dedicatory: Lines 39–40. "If my Success wou'd move any other who has a happier Genius." Philips's wish did not come true until fifteen years later, when Charles Shadwell (son of Thomas the Poet Laureate) began to write comedies for the Dublin stage. Significantly, one of Shadwell's plays, *The Sham Prince*, is set around St Stephen's Green.

Prologue: Line 9. *"And talks of Time, Place, Action, and the Plot."* Popular knowledge of the so-called three unities was probably derived from John Dryden's *An Essay of Dramatic Poesy* (1668, 1684, 1693), and from Dryden's Prefaces to his plays. Philips may be flattering his Dublin audience somewhat, but in later years, certainly, Dublin had the reputation of devastating and vociferous audiences.

Prologue: Line 14. *"And damn the Poet for the Actor's dress."* Costumes were a problem from the earliest days of Smock Alley. An eye witness describes *Othello* in November 1662: "We have Plays here in the newest Mode, and not ill acted; only the other Day, when OTHELLO was play'd, the DOGE OF VENICE and all his Senators came upon the Stage with Feathers in their Hats, which was like to have chang'd the Tragedy into a Comedy." Quoted La Tourette Stockwell, *Dublin Theatres and Theatre Customs (1637–1820)*, p. 27. The actors relied on their patrons for costumes, and the result was bound to be uncertain.

Prologue : Line 15. *"Strut in the Pit, Survey the Gallery."*
The Smock Alley theatre was constructed in the new mode,
i.e., with proscenium stage at one end of a rectangle, and an
auditorium comprising a pit (with benches), a row of boxes,
and galleries on three sides. The men often stood on the
benches in the pit, admiring the ladies about them. The
Dublin beau in *The Journal of a Dublin Beau* (1729) remarks
to his companions : "Why no One sure regards the *Play*, /
We'll ogle our *Half-Crown* away."

Prologue : Line 22. *"In the Box Blushes, or a Laugh above."*
The Smock Alley theatre was structured so as to accommodate
a division into classes; in total contrast to the Elizabethan
conditions, the lowest class was now highest up.

ACT I

SCENE *St Stephen's-Green.* Smock Alley shared with its London theatres royal, the new style of staging plays by means
of painted, changeable scenery. Records show that by the
sixteen seventies the theatre had amassed a considerable store
of stock scenery (William Smith Clark, *The Early Irish Stage*).
These would be background views and locations painted on
two large flats or "shutters", meeting in the centre. Whenever
a change of scene was called for, the flats would be replaced
by two others, slid in from each side on wooden grooves. Side
wings and borders completed the illusion of depth.

I.i.3. "To Pray for an Easterly Wind." That is, from England.
Whether sailing from Chester, Holyhead or Bristol, the visitor
from England had often to wait for prevailing winds. Cf.
Swift's lines, "Holyhead. Sept. 25. 1727" :

> Before, I always found the wind
> To me was most malicious kind
> But now, the danger of a friend
> On whom my fears and hopes depend . . .
> With rage impatient makes me wait
> A passage to the land I hate.

I.i.10–11. "A Mask in the Play-House." As Samuel Pepys testifies, masks began to be worn at the London theatres immediately after the Restoration. (See A. M. Nagler, *A Source Book in Theatrical History*.) The idea of sparing a woman's blushes soon altered to concealing an interesting lady's identity. By process of metonymy, mask or vizard quickly came to mean 'loose woman', as, for example, in Etherege's *The Man of Mode* (1676). Philips testifies that Dublin customs were no different from those in London.

I.i.15. "Than our Gallery does the Parson." The sort of in-joke customary among Restoration playwrights, for whom the theatre and the world of the town were freely interchangeable. In Dublin, as in London, the clergy were critical of the theatre in the sixteen nineties. In 1700 one preacher referred to "those nurseries and schools of wickedness, the Play houses, places the Devil claimeth as his own." The galleries, however, continued to support the theatre.

I.i.33–4. "I struggled harder to conceal my Flame, than to restrain my Heart." This conflict lies at the centre of most Restoration comedies. Art and nature were constantly in tension, prompting the cultivation of an appropriate style or set of "manners".

I.i.40–2. "No Estate, and a Fine Gentleman! Advise him to keep where he is, if he would preserve that Character." A significant modification of the usual cynicism underlying Restoration comedy. Whereas it is common for the Restoration hero to keep a sharp eye on the heroine's fortune, and to be cautious over his own, Philips points out that in Dublin character and money are synonymous. Cf. II.i.197–200, where the fop Vainly "has one Qualification will make many Men, and most Women value him . . . A Good Estate."

I.i.54–6. "To call for my Glass Chariot . . . Conquests." Marina here lists the main social outlets in Restoration Dublin. These were similar to London pastimes, with perhaps more emphasis on 'visiting', a custom which may have had something to do with Dublin's reputation as a gossip-loving town.

I.i.81–2. "So many Stait Fellows in Red out of Employment." Dublin was strongly garrisoned, and at this time peace reigned following the wars 1689–1692.

I.i.113. "See that our Things are brought from Ship-board." Visitors from England usually disembarked at Ringsend, two miles east of Trinity College.

I.i.126–7. "I dread it as much as our Farmers do the Wool-Bill." A very topical reference. William Molyneux's pamphlet, *The Case of Ireland's Being Bound by Acts of Parliament in England Stated*, appeared in 1698 (see the Cadenus Press edition, Dublin, 1977). The Wool Bill, prohibiting the export of wool from Ireland, was then pending, and Molyneux indicated by a remark in his Preface that he had this act in mind : "I have not any Concern in Wooll, or the Wooll-Trade." The act was passed in 1699 and was regarded as a major grievance, leading to the growth of Protestant nationalism. See J. C. Beckett, *The Making of Modern Ireland 1603–1923* (London, 1966), pp. 155–7.

I.i.173. "Beauty without Art or Affectation." Affectation was a cardinal error in the view of Restoration writers of comedy. The characterization of the fop was based on a recognition of the difference between art and affectation. Congreve, in his essay "Concerning Humour in Comedy" (1696) distinguishes between humour (shows us as we are), habit (shows us as we appear) and affectation (shows us as we would like to be under a "Voluntary Disguise"). It is clear that Congreve places humour highest, and finds it in nature or life itself. Philips echoes that sentiment.

I.i.209. "A half Crown Ordinary." A tavern where a meal, or ordinary, would be served at the not inexpensive rate of half a crown. The number of taverns and ale houses in Dublin is given as 1,500 in the minutes of the Corporation for 1667; there were hardly less in 1699. See Edward Mac-Lysaght, *Irish Life in the Seventeenth Century: After Cromwell* (Dublin, 1939).

I.i.230–6. "I have brought over some New Fashions," etc. An early example of the dependence of Dublin on whatever was in vogue in London. Cf. Jonathan Swift, *A Proposal for the Universal Use of Irish Manufacture* (1720): "the Biass among our People in favour of *Things, Persons,* and *Wares* of all Kinds that come from *England*."

I.i.246. *"This House is Infected with the Plague."* During the Cromwellian period Ireland suffered more deaths from plague than from the wars, but the epidemic which devastated London in 1665 was not so seriously felt in Ireland. (See MacLysaght, *Irish Life in the Seventeenth Century*.) Smallpox and dysentery (flux) were the common 'plagues' in Dublin.

I.i.305–6. "Pray let your Simile be short." A surprising anticipation of Millamant's "Dear Mr Witwoud, truce with your similitudes," *The Way of the World*, II.v.15. Congreve's play was staged in March 1700.

I.i.326–8. "Women of the Town! . . . why, there are no such things in this Town." This sentiment was still in existence in 1926 when Sean O'Casey's depiction of Rosie Redmond in *The Plough and the Stars* drew indignant response from Dubliners. In contrast, there is the testimony of John Dunton in *The Dublin Scuffle* (1699): "Tho' Whores are whipt every Sessions, (I saw seven but yesterday capering before the Beadle) yet the Prostitutes here are such very Prostitutes, that I heard Mr. Y—— say (*an old Fornicator in this City*) that tho' he had spent his Estate on a Whore in *Dublin*, that his Rival no sooner appeared, but she clung to the best Chapman. In this case . . . *he that bids most is the Buyer*." Smock Alley reputedly got its name from the trade carried on there.

I.i.437–9. "She has done more harm to deserving young Ladies Reputations, than the Small Pox has to their Faces." The disease most general in Ireland around 1700 was smallpox. "It was often fatal . . . it left its mark on high and low . . . and disfigured many a young seventeenth century beauty" (Edward MacLysaght, *Irish Life in the Seventeenth Century*, p. 213, n. 41). Cf. Mrs Hardcastle, "I vow, since inoculation

began, there is no such thing to be seen as a plain woman,"
She Stoops to Conquer (1773), II.i.

I.i.464–5. "Will you please to Dine with us at the *Globe.*"
Either the "Globe" tavern on Cork Hill, which was in exis-
tence until 1729, or the "Globe" coffee-house in Essex Street
(close to the theatre). Since Sir Francis refers to "the Coffee-
House" at II.i.299 it would appear to be the "Globe" coffee-
house that is meant. Later, in the reign of George II, this
"Globe" was the haunt of Dublin politicians. (See Gilbert,
History of the City of Dublin, II, 161–4.)

ACT II

II.i.45–8. "For that abundance of Powder in thy Perrewig?
or for neatly Twisting that great Slabbering Bib? or for the
nice Rowl of your Stockings? or for your Muff-String and
the Buckle?" These are all significant details of contemporary
dress. The periwig was adopted by the English court in 1664,
but powder did not come into general use until the 1690s.
(See James Laver, *A Concise History of Costume*, London,
1969, pp. 121–2.) The 'bib' was a steinkirk cravat which came
into vogue in 1692. The 'nice Rowl' : it became fashionable
c. 1690 for men to roll the tops of their stockings on the outside of their breeches. The 'Muff String' went around the
neck and held the muff in place at hip level in front. (Information supplied by Diana de Marly, Courtauld Institute.)
The prototype for this dandified character was Etherege's Sir
Fopling Flutter, whose wardrobe was conspicuously French.
Vainly also dresses "as if you were newly return'd from *Paris*"
(line 54).

II.i.60–2. "Such a Friend is an inestimable Jewel . . . so plain
dealing an Acquaintance." The wording suggests the influence
of Wycherley. In *The Country Wife* (1675) Horner says,
"plain dealing is a jewel" (IV.iii), a line used verbatim by
Vainly III.i.205 below. The eponymous hero of Wycherley's
The Plain Dealer (1676) gave currency to the phrase.

II.i.96. "An Antick, I suppose." A grotesque pageant or theatrical representation (*O.E.D.*). By the sound of it, the antic was then a popular sort of dance, probably disruptive of the "Ball" mentioned at line 98.

II.i.113. "Wondrous great." Possibly a usage derived from the Irish phrase *mór le chéile*, 'great with one another'. The expression survived in Hiberno-English into the twentieth century. Cf. James Joyce, "The Dead", in *Dubliners*. Gretta Conroy says of the dead Michael Furey, "I was great with him."

II.i.187. "I attack'd his most sensible part." That is, Vainly's posterior. A pun, probably, is intended on 'sensible'.

II.i.239–40. "Nothing but old Fables and Romances." Wormwood seems to display his own acquaintance with romantic fiction here. The realistic novel was soon to rescue the reputation of fiction, with the arrival of Defoe.

II.i.241–2. "In this Age talk of Virtue and Sense!" Wormwood's materialistic viewpoint is probably only an exaggeration of contemporary cynicism.

II.i.256–7. "Is *French* Wine admitted yet?" That is, presumably, in the interlude in the wars between England and France in Holland. The Peace of Rijswijk was declared in 1697.

II.i.296. "Incontinently." Immediately (obsolete).

II.i.348–9. "Any thing tho' she were in a Stuff Riding-hood." 'Stuff' meant fabric—a woollen riding-hood, perhaps, suggesting lowly status. The meaning is clear : 'anything in a skirt.'

II.i.350–1. "*We that have Vigour . . . clean.*" The rhyming couplet suggests the end of a scene, but no new scene is indicated. The stage is, however, left bare at the exit of Sir Francis.

II.i.374. "A Man of Conscience." Conscience was never a feature of Restoration comedy in its heyday. After the mid 1690s, however, in response to a change in public taste, the rake hero began to speak in a new tone. The *locus classicus*

is in Cibber's *Love's Last Shift* (1696), act V, where at the
moment of truth the rake hero is smitten to the soul by the
purity of the woman he has seduced (who turns out to be his
wife). Farquhar bows to the times in *The Beaux' Stratagem*
(1707) when Aimwell's conscience will not allow him to go
through with his deceit of Dorinda.

II.i.550. "You Jarr like Man and Wife already." That is,
bicker. A witty touch anticipatory of Millamant's, "let us be
as strange as if we had been married a great while", *The Way
of the World*, IV.v.

II.i.553–4. "I must be making Experiments." A reminder
that Restoration comedy and the Royal Society flourished side
by side. Scientific experimentalism underlay much of the
libertinism of Restoration comedy, e.g., Horner to Lady
Fidget, "I desire to be tried only, madam", *The Country Wife*,
II.i. Cf. Bonamy Dobrée, *Restoration Comedy 1660–1720*
(Oxford, 1924), p. 22, "Restoration comedy . . . expressed, not
licentiousness, but a deep curiosity, and a desire to try new
ways of living."

ACT III

III.i.55–64. "You will exclaim against a standing Army before
a broken Officer", etc. The general drift of this passage defines
the character of Lady Volant as two-faced. Cf. Dryden's
satire of Buckingham, "A man so various that he seemed to
be / Not one, but all mankind's epitome . . . Railing and
praising were his usual themes, / And both, to show his
judgment, in extremes", *Absalom and Achitophel*, vv. 545 ff.
    "A Fanatick before Papists, and with Fanaticks for *Iure
divino*." The term 'fanatic' was applied in the latter half of
the seventeenth century to Nonconformists as a hostile epithet
(*O.E.D.*). *Jure divino*: By divine right. The claim made for
the Stuart kings. Thus, 'Nonconformist among Jacobites'.

III.i.127. "Without the Garniture of a Patch, or a Sword-
knot." Face patches were decorative shapes stuck on the face,
e.g. stars, moons. A swordknot was a bow tied round the hilt
for decoration.

III.i.255. "Plenty of all sorts of Fish and Flesh." Philips's father also found time in his pamphlet, *The Interest of England in the Preservation of Ireland* (1689) to rhapsodize about the fish, rivers and lakes of Ireland.

III.i.404. "Romantick Sir." The earliest recorded usage is 1659, but the sense in which Philips uses 'romantic', "readily influenced by the imagination", is not recorded before 1700 (*O.E.D.*).

III.i.408. "A very ugly, ungentile Man." Ungenteel (obsolete).

III.i.458-62. "Twice in one week at the Play?" etc. It is implied that theatregoing was popular in Dublin c. 1699, and fashionable. For a lady to wear a mask in the gallery was *risqué*, and to sit in the pit was debarred until the middle of the eighteenth century. To be seen too often in St Stephen's Green may have been injurious to a lady's reputation, but Lady Volant is willing to meet Bellmine there in a mask.

ACT IV

IV.i.17-23. "I have observ'd that none Despise *Ireland* so much as those who thrive best in it." The first of many such criticisms to appear in Irish plays. Perhaps the best-known sequel is Charles Macklin's attack in *The True-born Irishman* (1762), through the satire of the Anglophile Mrs Diggerty.

IV.i.55. "I attended him to *Flanders*." A reference to the war of the coalition (England and the Netherlands) with France, brought to a temporary halt by the Peace of Rijswijk in 1697.

IV.i.60-1. "I had the humility to dispense with the Title of Captain." Philips's own rank. This passage has about it the ring of social observation. It is not the sort of detail commonly found in Restoration comedy.

IV.i.71-2. "She first apprehended the Cheat." Discovered the deception.

IV.i.275. "The Honour of a Pimp is sacred." A witticism with a proverbial ring to it.

IV.i.312. "One of your Mistresses." It was common for the hero of a Restoration comedy to be profligate, e.g. Dorimant is a three-timer (as opposed to a two-timer) in *The Man of Mode*, and Valentine provides for his bastard while consumed by love for Angelica in *Love for Love*. The fact that Marina is present for Trickwell's remark and makes no comment is significant. Cf. V.i.189, a reference to a "Fine Lady" kept by Bellmine in Covent Garden.

IV.i.317–8. "As punctual to me, as a Sharper wou'd be to a young Rich Cully he had Set." A sharper, a cheat or confidence man. Cully, "one who is cheated or imposed upon (e.g. by a sharper, strumpet, etc.); a dupe, gull; one easily deceived or taken in; a silly fellow, simpleton. (Much in use in the 17th c.)." *O.E.D.*

IV.i.320. "Miss the *Strand* on a *Sunday*." The Strand, made a fashionable resort by Ormond, held a part in Dublin social life comparable to Hyde Park in London. A Prologue referring to the closure of Smock Alley following the death of Charles II mentions "Crowded Green and Strand, but Empty Pit". See William Smith Clark, *The Early Irish Stage*, p. 94. See also note to Epilogue, line 17, below.

IV.i.367–70. "For 'tis as unreasonable for Women to expect Love after enjoyment . . . possession." The kind of cynical aphorism to be expected from the rake hero. Cf. Dorimant, "Th' extravagant words they speak in love. 'Tis as unreasonable to expect we should perform all we promise then, as do all we threaten when we are angry." *The Man of Mode*, V.ii.

IV.i.371. "What is that you mutter of unconscionable?" The aside convention, whereby the other characters on stage do not hear what the audience hear, is breached here. A sophisticated touch. Cf. V.ii.8–9.

IV.i.392. "No, that will not be so proper." Philips is careful to preserve the decorum of his two heroines. That the concept was already old-fashioned is suggested by Congreve's satire of Lady Wishfort, "I shall never break decorums", etc., in *The Way of the World*, III.v.

ACT V

V.i.3. "Wou'd it were a little darker however." A reminder that performances were still reliant mainly upon natural lighting at this time. A play started about 4 p.m. Candles and oil "floats" in the footlights provided extra light, but these, obviously, were not amenable to the control modern audiences are accustomed to.

V.i.9. "A Man of Honour." Cf. the repeated reference by Lady Fidget to her "honour" in *The Country Wife*, a play familiar to Dublin audiences. (See W. R. Chetwood, *A General History of the Stage*, Dublin, 1749.)

V.i.73–4. "And leave my Wealth to erect Hospitals to maintain Mad men and Fools." An anticipation of Swift's famous testament, "He gave the little wealth he had / To found a house for fools and mad." But the allusion may have been topical : in June–July 1699 Dr Thomas Molyneux introduced a proposal in the House of Commons for building a hospital "for the reception of aged lunaticks and other diseased persons, there being noe citty in the world soe considerable as this citty of Dublin where there is not some such." On behalf of a gentleman who wished to be nameless, Molyneux offered £2,000 towards the maintenance, and asked the city to contribute £200 to build on land outside St James's Gate given by the Earl of Athlone. See John T. Gilbert, *Calendar of Ancient Records of Dublin*, VI, 214.

V.i.85–6. "The value of a Rapparee Farthing." Another topical reference. The rapparees were armed bands made up mainly of ex-soldiers from the Jacobite armies "whose exploits were a dangerous combination of patriotism and brigandage." (J. C. Beckett, *The Making of Modern Ireland 1603–1923*, p. 150.) George Philips, the playwright's father, wrote to Lord Capel in 1694 in complaint of "those develish sort of men called Tories, or Rapparees." Coinage was in a "state of hopeless confusion" at this time (Edward MacLysaght, *Irish Life in the Seventeenth Century*) and the rapparees may have been partly to blame. Philips's father goes on to say in his letter : "The laws at present in force are not extensive enough against counterfeiting and clipping of true coin, or bringing in of false" (*Historical Manuscripts Commission. Report of the Manuscripts of the Duke of Buccleuch and Queensberry*, II, Part I, p. 105.) By Gresham's law, the brass money issued by James in 1689 led to the disappearance from circulation in Ireland of silver and gold. (See Richard Bagwell, *Ireland Under the Stuarts*, III, 277.)

V.i.141–2. "As much as a Man may improve himself in Conversation, by Drinking with the silent Club here." An obscure reference.

V.i.155–6. "Is the hopeful Son expell'd the Colledge?" With students from nearby Trinity College in attendance at the theatre such an allusion would doubtless be topical. Philips's fellow-Derryman George Farquhar was once one of those expelled (for a time) in 1696.

V.ii. *The Scene Changes.* This is the only such stage direction in *St Stephen's Green*, although the scene had changed earlier to Lady Volant's house (III.i.).

V.ii.5–6. "Because the Drums and Trumpets will Disturb us early." St Stephen's Green was used in Restoration times as an exercise ground for the garrison. (C. Litton Falkiner, *Essays Relating to Ireland Biographical Historical and Topographical*, London, 1909, p. 155.)

V.ii.26–7. "A Dialogue. / Set by Mr. LEVERIDGE." Richard Leveridge (c. 1671–1758) was a bass singer and a minor composer. He sang one of the leads in Purcell's *The Indian Queen* in London in 1695, and collaborated with Daniel Purcell and Jeremiah Clarke on *The Island Princess*, an opera staged at Drury Lane in November 1698. It was Leveridge and not Matthew Locke (as was long believed) who composed the music for Davenant's version of *Macbeth*, first staged in 1702 and thereafter staged all through the century. Leveridge also composed popular music, e.g., "The Roast Beef of Old England". (See Roger Fiske, *English Theatre Music in the Eighteenth Century*, London, 1973, pp. 26–9). Leveridge fled

London for Dublin for one year in 1699 in order to escape his creditors, a detail which helps to confirm the date of *St Stephen's Green* (See William Smith Clark, *The Early Irish Stage*, p. 114). The dialogue here was probably by Philips, Leveridge setting it to music, the continuo, i.e. a bass line played by both a stringed instrument and a harpsichord. It is noteworthy that the music-room at Smock Alley was still over the stage, as John Dunton testifies in *The Dublin Scuffle* (1699). T. J. Walsh seems a little confused on this point, in *Opera in Dublin 1705–1797* (Dublin, 1973), pp. 2, 47.

V.ii.177. "Beg'd an Estate of Forfeited Lands." As mistress to a court favourite Lady Volant might have acquired property in Ireland confiscated in the recent Jacobite wars. It may be possible to see here a veiled reference to Elizabeth Villiers, mistress of king William III, who gained over 95,000 acres of confiscated land in Ireland. In any event, the reference is topical, as the Commission of Inquiry sat in 1699 and the Act of Resumption (of forfeited lands) was passed in 1700. See J. G. Simms, *The Williamite Confiscation in Ireland 1690–1703* (London, 1956), pp. 82–121.

V.ii.205–6. "No, no, Sir, I am none of her Lovers, for I am her Husband." An early example of an Irish bull?

V.ii.254. "Pleasure and Freedom in a Goal." That is, in jail. A common spelling at this time.

V.ii.264–6. "A pretty Present . . . Twenty thousand Pounds ready Money." The mechanics of sentimental comedy are visible already here : virtue is never its own reward in post-Restoration drama. This development led to Goldsmith's complaint in his "An Essay on the Theatre; or, A Comparison between Laughing and Sentimental Comedy" (1773) that authors had become "lavish enough of their *tin* money on the stage". Philips may be seen as a transitional author, half way between the Restoration and the sentimental modes.

Epilogue : Line 17. "*Meet me at* Chappellizard, *or the* Strand." Chapelizod, a suburb of modern Dublin, well known to readers of *Finnegans Wake*. There was a royal castle here in the seventeenth century : King William stayed here after his victory at the Boyne. In the sixteen nineties the castle was the seat of the Lord Deputy, which may have given a certain attraction to the place. (See John D'Alton, *The History of the County of Dublin*. Dublin, 1838.)

The Strand was a fashionable promenade to the north-east of the city. John Dunton describes it as "a Mile from *Dublin*", and in characteristic style he found that it "gave me *a pleasant prospect of the Sea*, whose rowling Waves put me in mind of the Power of Omnipotence." Other visitors were doubtless put rather in mind of the Lady Volants of the day.